Hard Disk Solutions
with
Batch File Utilities

Hard Disk Solutions with Batch File Utilities

David D. Busch

BANTAM BOOKS
TORONTO • NEW YORK • LONDON • SYDNEY • AUCKLAND

HARD DISK SOLUTIONS WITH BATCH FILE UTILITIES
A Bantam Book / October 1987
2nd printing December 1987

All rights reserved.
Copyright © 1987 by David D. Busch.
Cover design copyright © 1987 by Bantam Books.
This book may not be reproduced or transmitted
in any form or by any means, electronic or
mechanical, including photocopying, recording
or by any information storage and retrieval
system, without permission in writing from the publisher.
For information address: Bantam Books.

ISBN 0-553-34409-9

Published simultaneously in the United States and Canada

Bantam Books are published by Bantam Books, a division of Bantam Doubleday Dell Publishing Group, Inc. Its trademark, consisting of the words "Bantam Books" and the portrayal of a rooster, is Registered in U.S. Patent and Trademark Office and in other countries. Marca Registrada. Bantam Books, 666 Fifth Avenue, New York, New York 10103.

PRINTED IN THE UNITED STATES OF AMERICA

B   11   10   9   8   7   6   5   4   3   2

Trademarks

IBM, IBM PC, IBM PC-XT, and IBM PC-AT are registered trademarks of International Business Machines Corporation.
Lotus *1-2-3* is a trademark of Lotus Development Corporation.
dBASE II and *dBASE III* are registered trademarks of Ashton-Tate.
Compaq is a registered trademark of Compaq Computer Corporation.
Microsoft, XENIX, and MS-DOS are registered trademarks of Microsoft Corporation.
CP/M is a registered trademark of Digital Research, Inc.
UNIX is a registered trademark of AT&T.
Tandy is a registered trademark of Tandy Corporation.
Seagate is a trademark of Seagate Technologies.

Contents

Preface   *ix*
Introduction   *xi*

Part One: Hard Disks Made Easy

1. *Mass-Storage Media*   **5**
2. *Hard Disk Basics*   **15**
3. *Why You Need a Hard Disk*   **29**
4. *Hard Disk Alternatives*   **35**
5. *Hard Disk Options*   **49**
6. *Tailoring Mass Storage to the Job at Hand*   **63**

Part Two: Hard Disk Tips and Tricks

7. *Getting Started*   **73**
8. *DOS*   **81**
9. *Tailoring Your Hard Disk*   **93**
10. *Getting DOS to Work for You*   **105**
11. *More DOS Tricks*   **123**
12. *Batch File Utilities*   **131**
13. *Advanced File Management Made Easy*   **153**

CONTENTS

14. Hard Disk Security **165**
15. A Hard Disk Menu System **177**
16. Hard Disk Backup Techniques **189**
Appendix A: Scan Codes **195**
Appendix B: Glossary **199**
Appendix C: Quick Guide to Using the Utilities **207**
Appendix D: Hard Disk Troubleshooting **211**

Preface

Imagine a world without hard disk drives for personal computers. It's difficult to visualize how we would be working today, because most of the recent innovations in personal computer hardware and software were made practical by the proliferation of the hard disk drive.

Without hard disk solutions to our data storage problems, most of us would be tied to clumsy software programs limited by frequent disk swapping. There would be no PC-based local area networks. Image-intensive office publishing would be constrained by bottlenecks in storing high-resolution bit-mapped data. Without hard disks, there would be no 80286 or 80386 microprocessors: why develop a more powerful chip when the data to keep that microprocessor busy is unavailable, or must be meted out in minuscule amounts?

Few components of a desktop computer other than the microprocessor chip itself can have more broad-reaching effects on convenience and productivity than a hard disk drive. Effective use of a hard disk can transform a personal computer from a sluggish business automation tool into a robust productivity booster. Properly equipped, a hard disk can help the user analyze information, make better decisions, and streamline tasks as mundane as word processing.

Those who have not used a hard disk regularly tend to think of it as a capacious replacement for a floppy disk, with room for 30 to 60 or more diskettes' worth of programs and data files. As you'll learn from this book, a hard disk can be so much more. Temporarily changing from one task to another can be accomplished almost instantly, with a near-seamless interface that allows for smooth, efficient workflow. Hard disks can place vast data files at our fingertips or allow for more sophisticated and powerful programs that would require tedious swapping of floppy disks. A hard disk can fortify and improve memory-resident utility programs, such as *Sidekick*, or keep vast dictionaries available for quick recall by spell-check or thesaurus aids. Hard disks can even function as cheap replacements for random-access memory (RAM), needed for mammoth Lotus spreadsheets, through one of the available "virtual memory" utilities that cause hard disk space to mimic the more expensive extended memory cards.

No other component of your computer system can affect as many other aspects in a positive way. In the near future, the 20-megabyte hard disk will become the standard minimum mass-storage component in all computers used in business, just as 256K of memory (512K in IBM PC-AT-compatible machines) has become the starting point for RAM. Learning to use hard disks effectively to solve business problems will simultaneously become a required skill for the computer-using professional.

Hard Disk Solutions is aimed at new users of hard disks who want a shortcut to proficiency. It is targeted at experienced hard disk veterans who want to pick up *new* tips that will help them get the most from their computers. With the accompanying software utilities, *Hard Disk Solutions* will streamline your work and show that multimegabyte storage doesn't have to be hard.

Introduction

IBM personal computers and compatibles equipped with a hard disk are rapidly becoming the standard configuration for business applications. According to *Future Computing*, 788,000 hard disks were sold bundled with computer systems in 1985, and another 483,000 hard disks were sold as add-on expansion products. Another million or two hard disk computers were sold in 1986 as the trend really took off.

Yet, until now, there have been no good, easily understood books on getting the most from a hard disk, aimed at a broad range of users. This book and accompanying software is aimed directly at present and future users of fixed disk drives. The text serves as a guide that will help PC users who want to wend through the confusion of selecting an aftermarket hard disk for their computers. Other chapters lead all hard disk owners through getting started and getting the most from their hard disks. Tips, tricks, and simple utilities make this package an in-depth guide to hard disk proficiency.

While the readers of this book will have different computers and configurations, it will be assumed that all of them are using their hard disks for business applications. So, in discussing hard disk use, the book will address the concerns of business users: using the hard disk with word processing, database, or spreadsheet programs; securing sensitive files; getting more work done by efficient hard disk management, etc.

Hard Disk Solutions includes very specific information on hard disk types, configuring the drives, and using them with DOS. However, it is not so dependent on current hardware, such as the IBM PC-XT, PS/2, or PC-AT, and software, such as DOS 3.3, as to become quickly outmoded when IBM and Microsoft introduce their move to OS/2 in the coming months. The information in this book will apply to all hard disk users now, and for several years to come.

Most other books that address hard disk concerns talk about the PC-XT and PC-AT as if they were the only hard disk option. Here, we'll present information of interest to those users, but will also answer questions of those who want to upgrade their IBM PC or compatible with an add-on hard disk drive. This book answers all the questions about hard disks for current and future owners. How will a hard disk benefit business and personal applications? Exactly what are the benefits of increased on-line storage? Besides just eliminating disk swapping, how will a hard disk streamline working methods and increase productivity? Those who may have been thinking of adding a hard disk will find out about the sticky "compatibility" problem; learn how to discover whether or not their internal power supply is up to the task; find tips on selecting an upgrade hard disk and getting it to work with other system components flexibly and efficiently. Once the reader has discovered how easy moving to hard disk is, the book presents a wealth of tips and tricks that make this mass-storage tool even more powerful.

The book shows how to redefine keys so that programs can be summoned at the press of a single key (Alt-W to load word processing, Alt-C for communications, Alt-S for spreadsheet, and so forth). This configuration can be automatically loaded each time DOS is booted—and includes tips on changing directories invisibly as the user moves smoothly from application to application. A complete, yet easy-to-understand discussion of tree-structured directories is included. The reader will learn how to construct useful batch files and "hide" them from view. DOS can be "told" how to find them through a simple PATH command included in the AUTOEXEC.BAT file. Simple utilities for creating, purging, and removing complex directory paths are also provided.

Special attention is given to the PC-AT, DOS 3.x, and the

future of hard disk computers as file servers in local area networks.

Why You Need Hard Disk Solutions

For the neophyte, a hard disk is the Australia of computer peripherals. Its resources are almost too huge to manage, and most users find they are familiar only with a few superficial aspects. Once they acquire a hard disk of their own, they find that they know far less about how to manage and use this tool than they had imagined.

A hard disk is much more than a huge, fast, floppy disk. Set up and maintained well, a hard disk can save time and provide powerful *new* capabilities. Mismanaged, a hard disk can be a bottomless pit into which software and data files disappear, never to be seen again. Bad planning and poor filing structures can cause the user to duplicate effort, waste space, and, in the worst cases, actually lose irreplaceable data.

Hard Disk Solutions will provide tips and tricks, compiled by a grizzled veteran of the computer wars, that will help you avoid making common mistakes and lead you to optimizing your use of what is currently the most popular and least understood computer accessory.

As a bonus, you'll become expert at using a broad range of DOS commands almost painlessly through the batch file utilities that are thoroughly described and commented upon.

Who Can Use This Book?

Hard Disk Solutions will appeal to a broad audience, including present owners of IBM PC-XT, PS/2, and PC-AT computers equipped with a factory-installed or add-on hard disk, as well as those with compatibles such as the Compaq II or Tandy 3000 HL who want to sharpen their hard disk management skills. We'll also address the needs of new owners of these computers who are puzzled with the complexity of hard disk management and want an easy-to-understand guide that leads

INTRODUCTION

them step-by-step through setting up a sophisticated hard disk system.

Finally, there will be much to interest potential hard disk users who want to read up on the technology before making a decision. Because of the plummeting cost of hard disks and the huge (7-million-plus) installed base of non-hard-disk PCs, these readers could equal the first two groups in number.

To benefit from this book you do not have to be a "power" user. Concepts will be introduced with thorough explanations, and will progress rapidly to more advanced levels to interest the more proficient reader. By the end of the book, any hard disk user should feel comfortable and confident with his or her new knowledge.

How to Use This Book and Software

The text is divided into two sections. Part one provides in-depth explanations of what hard disks are and how they work. Without getting overly technical, these chapters provide valuable information for those who can benefit from nuts-and-bolts explanations of hard disk options and alternatives. You'll find concise descriptions of other mass-storage devices, ranging from so-called Bernoulli-effect drives to optical disks and bubble memory. Here, you'll discover solid justification for adding a hard disk to your equipment array, and tips on sizing storage to meet the needs of the application at hand. Most readers will find that part one forms a basis for gaining complete hard disk proficiency.

This book is *not* a technical treatise, however. Some technical information is provided in the introductory chapters for those who want to know more about how hard disks work. It is not intended to be the last word in technical detail. Nor will we dwell on overly technical, highly product-specific facts, such as the fifteen or twenty or thirty different hard disk types that must be "specified" during installation. Different configurations of platters and tracks will *not* be the focus of this book.

If you don't *need* to understand the inner workings of the hard disk, or simply aren't interested in these technical topics, you may skip over the first part of this book. Part one can stand alone as a technical reference should you need it later.

Part two is an applications-oriented guide to streamlining hard disk operations. Chapters here cover everything from setting up and formatting the hard disk, to designing a simple-to-use menu system for the neophyte user. You'll also find several schemes for protecting your hard disk from unauthorized users, and a wealth of batch file utility programs. Explanations of how to use the utilities provided on the disk accompanying this book are also integrated into the text in part two.

However, if you want to take a shortcut and begin using the utilities right away, jump to Appendix C, which provides a quick guide to transferring software to your hard disk and putting it to work.

PART ONE
HARD DISKS MADE EASY

It is always useful to have a thorough understanding of something that can make such a difference in the way you work. While there have been highly technical works written about hard disks for the systems integrator, computer hobbyist, or electronics engineer, the *users'* guides to hard disks have been lacking in more in-depth information presented in a way that the average intelligent computer user can understand. The first six chapters of this book will provide a lot of the information you have wondered about but were unable to glean from reading magazines or other material.

In part one there will be a discussion of mass-storage concepts in general, some historical information on how the hard disk and other magnetic media developed, and a comparison between hard disks and your alternatives. We'll explain *why* you need a hard disk in the first place and outline some of the most frequent applications. Finally, the various hard disk options from hard disk cards to externally mounted systems will be covered, along with considerations in choosing what size hard disk is best for you.

1
Mass-Storage Media: Gateways to Personal Productivity

A desktop computer is a gateway to working smarter and faster. However, acting as sentry over that gateway are very strict "gatekeepers," limiting the type and quantity of information we can process and use.

There are many potential bottlenecks standing between us and personal computer productivity. However, four of these gatekeepers have received the most attention in recent years because of the crucial role they play. These include the microprocessor chip and its associated circuitry, the CRT display, the printer, and the computer system's mass-storage device. While the functions of each of these differ sharply, their gatekeeping roles share the common aspects of *speed* and *capacity*.

Central to any personal computer is the microprocessor, its associated circuitry, and the programming written for it. The microprocessor chip is the brain of the computer, containing temporary information storage locations, or *registers*, which are used to hold data while the computer adds to it or subtracts from it or uses the contents of the register to determine whether or not some other action is carried out. The microprocessor also has certain built-in *instructions* which can be called by the programming to perform various functions with the registers.

Everything a microcomputer does involves using the central microprocessor or supporting microprocessor in the system. For example, in addition to the "main" microprocessor in an IBM PC or compatible (typically an Intel 8088, 80286, or 80386 chip or some variation), a computer system may have an 8087 or 80287 math "coprocessor," as well as other microprocessors that handle graphics/display functions, memory management, or disk input-output (I/O).

If any of these microprocessors are slow or lack power, we are limited in the types of applications that can be handled practically. Programs that require much calculation are heavily dependent on processor speed and power—and that can encompass nearly every type of application, system program, or utility, from word processors to spreadsheets.

The software running on the microprocessor also plays a related gatekeeping role. A clumsy operating system or an inefficiently coded applications program can set a limit on the types and amount of work we can do. So-called reduced instruction set computers (RISC) use fast microprocessors with fewer different instructions available, and therefore depend heavily on efficient software for their power. Most computer users have some experience with computer systems that process information slowly, or software that seems to take forever to perform a given task. The microprocessor/software gremlin may be at work in such cases.

Less obvious at first glance may be the gatekeeping roles served by a personal computer's *monitor* or *printer*. These peripherals offer a host of limitations that can handicap our efficiency. Both restrict the type of information we can manipulate and reproduce either on the screen or in hard-copy form.

Early printers and monitors were once limited only to alphanumeric, or text, information. That is because the predominant form of information supplied to software the computers ran was in the form of text or numbers. There were, of course, specialized programs that used graphics or that converted real-world events to nonalphanumeric information, and back again (such as scientific or control interfaces with analog-to-digital or digital-to-analog converters). However, the majority of the first personal computer applications involved nothing more than text and numbers. So monitors didn't need to display anything other than alphanumerics, and printers had no need to print anything else.

More recently, we have begun supplying personal computers with different types of information. For example, it is possible to *scan* a piece of paper or a photograph and break the image down into individual picture elements, or *pixels*, that represent a graphic image of that document. Each pixel can be represented by a binary 1 or 0, depending on whether a dot or absence of a dot best represents the image information in that picture element. Because only a single bit is needed to represent each pixel, an 8-bit byte can represent 8 individual picture elements. By turning on or off the pixels on a CRT (cathode-ray tube) to match this "bit map" of the original image, we can portray graphics or photographs on a computer screen. (To be 100 percent accurate, it should also be noted that for *better* representation of an image, the *intensity* of each pixel should also be recorded. Some systems use an entire byte to represent the comparative intensity of a pixel and can thus include 256 different shadings, or gray tones. Continuous-tone or gray-scale imaging can take eight times as much memory and disk storage space as a binary pixel bit map.)

The larger the number of pixels that can be displayed on a CRT, the higher the resolution of the image. Thus, the design of the display screen and the graphics card that drives it can have a gatekeeping effect on the type of information we can handle.

Printers play an equivalent role in limiting our output, although printer resolution is typically higher than CRT resolution. Many dots reproduced by a laser or dot-matrix printer may represent a single screen pixel. In this way, various gray levels can be represented—by mixing more white spaces in with the solid black dots on the paper. Screen resolution for personal computers, even those outside the IBM arena, rarely exceeds 1,000 × 1,000 dots, nor printers much more than 400 dots per inch.

With monitors, the range of colors that can be reproduced generally falls far short of that which can be displayed on a simple color television set, while color printers are even more primitive. Lacking full-color, high-resolution images and printouts, applications from office publishing to image-intensive information management are severely limited by these twin gatekeepers.

Image-intensive information, as well as plain old alphanumeric data, are also overburdening our PC data storage systems. As a result, data storage is receiving lavish attention as a gatekeeper barring the path to improved productivity. After all, a typical 80286-based computer can execute instructions in a microsecond, while the average access time needed to retrieve a given block of data from a hard disk drive is 40 to 85 *milliseconds*. In other words, a hard disk is anywhere from 40,000 to 85,000 times slower than the microprocessor chip it serves. This is not strictly true, since other factors, such as the speed at which the computer's controller and input/output channels transfer the data, can limit a hard disk's ability to supply information at its top speed.

However, this disparity between how quickly data storage can be read or written and how quickly the microprocessor can handle it is nothing new. Data storage has always been a prime concern of both personal computer users and the manufacturers of equipment. The very earliest microcomputers of a decade ago had little or no data storage as we know it today. When such computers were powered up, their operators, who probably also built the computer from scratch or a kit, had to enter a tiny *bootstrap* program by throwing toggle switches on the front of the machine. Other software, including programming languages like BASIC, had to be slowly loaded through punched paper tape. When such a computer was switched off, all the data was lost, unless the user took the time to output memory contents to a paper tape.

Magnetic storage soon followed. There are basically two types of magnetic storage. One is called *serial* storage, in which the information is stored continuously over the length of the medium, such as tape. In the microcomputer world, serial storage using cassette tape and tape recorders has generally been slow and inconvenient to use. By roughly 1977, when the first ready-to-use personal computers like the Apple II, Radio Shack Model I, and Commodore Pet were introduced, cassette data storage was already destined to be used only for home and hobby computing. Personal computer minifloppy disk drives, and their rapid, random-access storage, first available in the late 1970s, became within a few years the standard media for information and programs.

After all, even the fastest tape systems designed for early personal computers were painfully strict gatekeepers. The simple software of the day could take five or ten minutes to load. Storing a small database back onto tape could take as long. Rapid access to information, and programs requiring such access, were totally out of the question. Early computers were limited to 64 kilobytes (K) of random-access memory, so there was little room in RAM for data storage.

Floppy disks literally made the personal computer as we know it today feasible. Disk drives are at least ten times faster than simple cassette tape storage devices. Programs could be loaded in seconds. In fact, very large programs that were too big to fit into 64K of memory could be written in segments, or *overlays*, that could be called into memory from disk when needed, replacing other parts of the program in RAM. Programs like *Wordstar* were designed in this way to bring new word-processing power to users of personal computers.

Data files could be as large as necessary for an application. Random-access file techniques made it possible to access any given record stored on disk quickly. The chief limitation was that of the capacity of the disk—or the number of disk swaps the user was willing to make in the course of the session. To a lesser extent, speed of access also became a consideration. A new corollary of Parkinson's law is always quickly applied to data storage: the amount of data that must be accessed always expands to fit the time in which the user is willing to wait for it.

By 1983, when IBM introduced its Personal Computer XT, the hard disk was ready to assume a position of a particularly magnanimous gatekeeper. Instead of 160K to 360K of program and information storage, a hard disk (also called, variously, fixed disk or rigid disk) offered 10 megabytes (MB)—or more—of space, with access four to ten times as fast. If the floppy disk made personal computers practical for business, the hard disk brought within reach mainframelike tools, utilities, and capabilities.

In fact, fast, high-density storage makes it possible to

improve the performance of the other three gatekeepers. Ultra-high-resolution displays and printers require prodigious amounts of storage to preserve their bit-mapped images. Faster microprocessors and more efficient software are of little import if they can't access the data they need to process.

A Historical Perspective

To better understand some of the technology behind the hard disk, it is useful to take a brief look at some of the data storage options that preceded it. Many readers will find this information of interest for historical reasons. Others will find that a recap provides them with a broader perspective that will be of value in gaining true hard disk proficiency.

Hard disks of today grew from technology developed for larger minicomputer and mainframe computer systems. Magnetic storage on such systems has a long and glorious history, dating from the serial tape drives still in use today and the first fixed and removable hard disk drives using what is called "Winchester" technology.

Flexible, or floppy, disks are actually a somewhat newer development. The original 8-inch floppy disks were intended as a temporary program transport medium which could be used to economically supply programs for computer systems. The first floppy disk drives were buried deep within the computer and not normally accessed by the end user.

However, 8-inch floppies, which could hold a megabyte of information, soon found their way into many systems, particularly dedicated word processors, as a program and data storage medium. Many early personal computers were equipped with floppy interfaces for 8-inch drives.

Such use of floppies continued even after the introduction of the 5¼-inch "minifloppy" diskette, because the newer format could store much less information. Apple II computers, for example, could manage only 143K of data on a single-sided diskette, while the first IBM Personal Computers upped the ante to no more than 160K bytes.

Today, 8-inch disks have fallen into disuse, and to many users the term *floppy* or *disk* means only the 5¼-inch minifloppy diskette. However, we also have 1.2 megabyte "high-capacity" 5¼-inch diskettes, and smaller 3½-inch "hard-shelled" disks that nevertheless store twice as much data as the standard floppy.

The standard IBM-type 5¼-inch floppy disk will be with us for many years to come, as primary storage for the 50 percent of computer users who will not have hard disks by the year 1990 (according to *Future Computing* estimates). Such disks will also continue to be used as a quick and easy way to exchange data between computers, and for backup.

The ubiquitous IBM-format diskette stores 180K of information on a single circular surface that measures, of course, 5¼ inches in diameter and is encased in a protective square jacket. Such diskettes are double-sided, providing a total of 360K of storage. The newer high-density diskettes introduced with the IBM Personal Computer AT store 600,000 bytes of data per side on special diskettes, for a total of 1.2 megabytes.

When 5¼-inch diskettes started enjoying wide use in the late 1970s, they were dubbed "minifloppies" or "minidisks" to differentiate them from the original 8-inch disks. The smaller 3½-inch disks logically were termed "micro disks." Today, the "mini" and "micro" terminology has generally been replaced by the simpler "5¼-inch disk" and "3½-inch disk" designations. Since "floppy disk" is now applied to both 5¼- and 8-inch diskettes, users frequently include the dimension when referring to the larger disks as well.

Most microcomputers sold in the past four or five years, including IBM and IBM compatibles, use 5¼-inch disks, with double-sided, double-density, soft-sectored disks being the most popular. Some of the newest microcomputers, particularly the laptops and the latest generation of desktop computer from IBM, use the more compact 3½-inch disks.

Each disk is coated on both sides with a magnetic material that is related to the coatings on audiotape or video recording tape. Manufacturing flexible disks is a multistep, complex process. First, large rolls of the polyester support, called the *substrate,* are produced. Magnetic particles, usually ferric oxide, possibly doped with cobalt, are manufactured, and then mixed with adhesives and solvents.

The magnetic mixture is next rolled onto the substrate in

a process that is very similar to producing photographic film, except that only a single layer is coated, compared to the more complex multilayer coatings used for film. During coating, the particles are exposed to conflicting magnetic fields in order to randomize them. So-called web coating is the most common procedure, but manufacturers have been experimenting with "spin coating," which has been used only for rigid disks but provides a more uniform, higher-density magnetic coating.

Calendering, where the coating is pressed evenly onto the substrate, is followed by *curing.* Next, the baked rolls are slit into narrower rolls and disks are punched from them. The disk "cookies" are then smoothed and polished, and a hub ring added to reinforce the center holes.

Once the disks have been inserted in their protective jackets, they are certified. During this step, the disk is tested for reliability. Depending on the outcome of this process, the disk will be certified as single- or double-sided, and single, double, or quad density. Following certification, the disk jackets are top sealed, labeled, enveloped, and boxed.

In use, the computer information is encoded on one or both sides of the disk by the read/write heads (which are electromagnets) of the disk drive.

There are several important differences between computer diskettes and audio recording tape, however. Conventional analog audiotape recordings consist of a range of frequencies and amplitude ("volume") information. Computer information is stored only in digital form. That is, the binary code (the 1's and 0's that the computer understands) is put on the diskette. So, instead of amplitude information, computer magnetic media are concerned only with the reversals of the direction of the magnetic particles on the disk. These changes in magnetic orientation are called *flux changes.* Like audiotape, magnetic disks can be reused by recording new information over the old.

While the recording and playback techniques are roughly similar, audiotape is not really analogous to diskettes for other reasons. Tape is a serial, or *sequential,* recording medium. In use, the tape moves from one reel to another, passing by the magnetic heads. We always retrieve the information at the beginning of the tape first, and cannot get to the information at the end of the tape without first transporting the entire length of the tape from one reel to another.

With audio recordings, this is not a drawback. It becomes an inconvenience only when we want to jump from one song to another within the tape rapidly, in a random sequence. Even with fast-forward and reverse mechanisms, it can take several seconds to a minute or more to move from one selection to another on a tape.

Flexible disks use a random-access method that might be compared to the way a record player accesses individual songs on a phonograph album. Read/write heads in a disk drive are located on a movable carriage assembly, which can be stepped out to any place where desired information is located, like the tonearm on a record player. A flexible diskette has 40, 80, or more concentric tracks. Because the read/write head can move from one track to another so quickly, far less time is needed to access any desired piece of information.

Actually, the audio compact disk is much more analogous to the flexible or hard disk because, unlike a phonograph record where the information is stored in one long, continuous groove, compact disk information, floppy disk data, and data stored on hard disks are arranged in discrete tracks. In fact, the compact disks we use for music are actually nothing more than optical disk media that can be used with equal ease for computer information.

The flexible media of a floppy diskette could be damaged by rough handling or foreign substances. Therefore, diskettes are placed in a protective jacket. To enable the read/write head to access the media, 8-inch and 5¼-inch diskettes have an oblong, rounded hole cut through the jacket to expose part of the disk surface. The hard-jacketed 3½-inch diskettes have a sliding metal cover that retracts once the disk has been inserted in the drive.

When the disk is in the drive, a two-piece mechanism clamps down on each side of the central hole to rotate the disk. Because of the slight possibility of damage from frequent use of a disk, a plastic *hub ring* is often included to reinforce the center hole of the diskette. The problem does not exist at all with 3½-inch disks, which have a metal circle in the center that provides a notch for the disk drive mechanism to turn.

As the disk rotates in the drive, the read/write head scans various tracks for information. The 8-inch and 5¼-inch disks generally have a smaller hole located a short distance from the center hole, through which a light shines to a detector, marking the starting point of each track. Some disks, not used with IBM computers, are *hard-sectored;* that is, they have a series of holes arranged in a ring around the center, permanently marking individual sections, or *sectors,* within a track. The individual sectors of the track in IBM-style *soft-sectored* disks are delineated by magnetic information written on the track when the disk is first set up, or *formatted,* for use.

The software knows where the beginning of each program or data file is stored from the disk's *directory,* a special part of the disk that is updated each time information is written on the disk. The directory tells the disk drive where to move the read/write head to reach a given file's starting sector and begin reading.

Most disk drives find a given track simply by moving the disk head a prescribed distance from the disk's center or edge. High-precision "stepper" motors position the head with sufficient accuracy to find a track. This is true even though conventional flexible diskettes can have as many as 96 tracks in a single inch of the radius of a disk.

However, newer technologies now are allowing manufacturers to produce read/write heads and higher "density" recording media that permit information to be even more tightly packed, as much as 10 megabytes on a single 5¼-inch diskette. For these, a special method is used to mark the tracks. The disks are preformatted at the factory with magnetic information that marks both sides of each track with a code. A pair of codes set off each sector and are used by a servomechanism in the drive to keep the head in the optimum position.

This has been a brief introduction to the world of magnetic mass storage. In the next chapter we'll look at some of the specialized technologies that had to be developed in order to make it possible to record and read more information, much more quickly, with a hard disk drive.

2
Hard Disk Basics

A hard disk resembles the floppy disk in that a circular magnetic surface is used to record information. However, the media, read/write heads, other drive components, interface circuitry, and sometimes a controller are incorporated in one compact unit. This integration allows a higher degree of precision in matching components that make up the hard disk drive, and hence permits some special techniques that result in much higher information densities.

Instead of a flexible polyester substrate for the magnetic coating, fixed disk drives use a rigid aluminum platter. Hard disks small enough to be mounted internally in IBM and compatible computers first used 5¼-inch platters; today, more compact 3½-inch hard disks offer the same, or greater, capacity and have even made it possible to fit a hard disk onto a card that will fit into a single expansion slot.

Hard disks use the same basic principle of the floppy: information is recorded on a disk-shaped magnetic surface by a read/write head which causes changes in the magnetic orientation of the particles on the surface. The basic information-recording techniques used both for floppy and hard disks are similar. Before the data is recorded, all the magnetic particles on the disk are aligned in the same direction. As information is written, electric currents in the read/write head produce appropriate flux changes in the magnetic orientation of these particles. When the data is read back, these changes in the disk *induce* electrical currents in the read/write head, producing electrical signals that can be amplified and interpreted by the controller and passed on to the computer system.

The distance between these flux changes on the disk determine the density of information that can be recorded on the disk. The distance can be measured radially out from the center of the disk (how many different tracks can fit on the disk, or tracks per inch), as well as along the path of the track itself (bits per inch).

In floppy disk drives, the diskette rotates at about 300 RPM, and the read/write heads actually touch the surface of the disk. Hard disk drives achieve their greater capacity and speed through a much headier rotational speed of roughly 3,600 RPM, and a "floating" read/write head that is supported by the resulting cushion of air.

Because even a particle of dust can loom as an impassable object given the low "flying height" of a hard disk read/write head, the platters and heads must be sealed inside a mini "clean room" that provides an environment free of contaminants. If this protection is breached, the user is exposed to the dreaded "head crash." A grain of dust, or sometimes external vibration, can cause the read/write head to strike the disk platter forcefully instead of gliding over smoothly. Should the head crash take place when the head is passing over an information-containing area, data can be permanently lost. In the worst cases, damage can occur in the directory track, whereupon the disk controller no longer knows where to find *any* of the information on the disk.

With a hard disk, smaller read/write heads are used, allowing data to be packed much more tightly together on the disk. A floppy disk may consist of nine sectors per track, each holding 512 bytes of information, recorded at a 48-tracks-per-inch density along the radius of the diskette. By contrast, a hard disk may contain 345 tracks per inch, each with 17 or 18 sectors.

For simplicity's sake, in the discussion that follows, we'll talk about the hard disk as if it consisted of a single platter with a single surface on which have been recorded magnetic tracks and sectors. In truth, hard disks generally have several platters, each with two surfaces, and read/write heads mounted in sets that read all the corresponding tracks of all the surfaces on all the platters simultaneously. Because this arrangement provides a *cylinder* of tracks, one on top of each other, a common way of referring to a hard disk's physical makeup is in terms of these cylinders. However, as we'll see, the physical layout of a hard disk may or may not have anything to do with how the hard disk controller and your computer view the *logical* arrangement of the disk.

Physical features are those that have some reality in a material sense: a hard-sectored floppy disk has physical sectors. A hard disk that has been formatted also has physical sectors and tracks in the sense that concrete magnetic information has been written defining exactly where those tracks and sectors begin and end. The computer can't change the arrangement of the tracks and sectors simply by interpreting them differently.

Logical features are those that are imaginary in the sense that they exist only because we or the computer system chooses to treat them as such. A data file is a logical collection of information, because, to the computer, the sectors that make up a data file are no different than random information that might also be written to a disk. We choose to tell the computer to retrieve all these particular sectors when we ask for a given data file, because they logically fit together to meet our information needs.

We'll encounter some examples of logical and physical features throughout this book. Cylinders are a logical way of thinking about a physical collection of "stacked" tracks, for example.

Factors Affecting Hard Disk Speed

There are four major physical factors that affect how quickly a hard disk can write or read data. These are cylinder size, data transfer rate, access time, and average latency.

Cylinder Size

Cylinder size is obviously determined by the number of surfaces or platters in a hard disk. The more surfaces, the larger the cylinder, and the more data that can be read by the multiple heads in a given period of time.

Data Transfer Rate

Data transfer rate is the rate at which data comes off the disk; it can be affected by the rotation speed of the disk, bit density, and a factor called *sector interleaving.*

At 3,600 RPM, each revolution of the disk takes about 1/60 of a second, but reading a full track of information generally takes longer. That is because the information on each track passes under the read/write head generally at a faster pace than the controller can receive, decode, and pass it along to the computer system. After reading sector 1, the controller must process that information and transmit it to the computer. However, the next physical sector on the hard disk is written immediately following the first, so the controller may not be ready to read that next sector.

One solution would be to have the read/write head *wait* until the disk made another entire revolution to bring the next physical sector into position. This would mean that it might require 17 revolutions to read an entire track. More commonly, hard disk systems alternate, or interleave, the sectors on a track. The sector that the controller *logically* sees as sector 2 may in fact be the fifth sector on the track. It will read sector 1, process that information, then read sector 5, process that information, and read sectors 10 and 15 on a single revolution of the disk. Then, the controller will skip sectors 16 and 17, as well as sector 1 when the beginning of the track comes around again, and read the *second* sector on the disk—beginning the skipping process all over again. Instead of taking seventeen revolutions to read a track, this process allows reading the entire track in only five revolutions.

The number of tracks that must be skipped to provide read reliability is called the *interleave factor.* The first IBM disk drives used an interleave factor of 6:1. Modern hard disks may use a factor of 4:1 or 3:1, or higher, depending on how fast they can process information. Keep in mind that setting an interleave factor that is too high can be as detrimental to performance as setting one that is too low. If a hard disk can't

HARD DISK BASICS

keep up with the information it is trying to read, it will have to wait for an entire revolution for that track to come around again—$\frac{1}{60}$ of a second, or almost 17 milliseconds. If this happens often enough, the consequences can be must more significant than the mere millisecond or two lost each revolution skipping sectors.

As described, the speed with which a hard disk is able to supply information to the computer depends on factors such as the rate with which the drive is able to read information from a single track, the interleave factor which determines how many revolutions are needed to read that track, and the time it takes for the read/write head to move from one track to another. If a hard disk is able to read or write an entire track with seventeen 512-byte sectors in a single revolution (that is, an interleave factor of 1:1), it will handle 17 × 512 bytes, or 8,704 bytes of information in a single $\frac{1}{60}$-second revolution. That translates into a transfer rate of 5 megabits per full second (8,704 bytes × 10 bits/byte × 60). This is an effective top limit on the speed with which data can be read from the hard disk. The only way to increase the transfer rate beyond 5 MBits/second is to speed up the disk platter, or to pack more information into each track, thereby providing more sectors.

Access Time

The effective rate at which information is generally read is slower, not only because of the interleave factor, but because of the need to move the read/write head between tracks. This *access time* includes the amount of time it takes to move the read/write heads over the specific track on the disk to be read/write. Once the heads have been placed at that track, they must settle down from the moving height to the height used for reading and writing. "Settling" time is normally included in the access time figures provided for a disk drive.

Average Latency

Once a head has finished seeking and settling, the disk drive controller must wait until the desired track spins the rest of the way around to the first sector before the read or write can

19

actually take place. This nonproductive period is called *latency*. Since this period will sometimes be very short, when only a few sectors remain before the start of the track, and other times much longer, when the disk must spin around almost the entire distance, an average latency figure corresponds to *half* the time needed for the drive to spin around. For hard disks which spin at 3,600 RPM, the average latency is 8.33 milliseconds.

These access speeds are commonly measured in terms of the average time needed to reach any given track on the disk. If the read/write head is located above track 1, it will obviously take less time to move from there to track 150 than to track 317. However, the track-to-track access time is generally given as the time needed to move from the edge of the disk to the center track, as the actual time needed will average out to this over many disk accesses. Access times can range from an average of 85 milliseconds (about $\frac{1}{12}$ of a second, or five full revolutions of the hard disk!) to 28 milliseconds or less.

Since 85 milliseconds is about three times as long as 28 milliseconds, the time needed to move from one track to another can have as great an impact on hard disk speed as the data transfer rate or interleave factor. In providing high-performance hard disks for modern computers, manufacturers have attempted to make improvements in all three areas. Disk drives are built to operate with 1:1 interleave factors, and with an even lower track-to-track access time.

Packing information more tightly within a track increases the number of 512-byte sectors that can be written to the track, and thus improves the data transfer time. However, it makes little sense to pack information closer together if the read/write heads are unable to read or write the information reliably, or if the controller is unable to process the data.

Disk Controllers and Interfaces

A device interface is a standardized way of communicating between two components, in this case the hard disk drive and the computer system. There are a number of standard and quasi-standard interfaces between hard disks (and other peripherals) and IBM PCs and compatible computers. The ST506/412 interface has been one of the most popular.

The interface was named after the Seagate Technologies 6-megabyte ST506 and its 12-megabyte successor, the ST412, which offer formatted capacities of 5- and 10-megabytes, respectively. It is what is called a *device-level* interface. In hard disks, such an interface links the controller and disk directly with a large collection of signal lines, each of which carries a separate value. Because the operation of the hard disk and the controller are so tightly linked together, such an interface can be very efficient when the two are well matched. On the other hand, to upgrade the performance of one, you frequently have to replace both.

Given a few changes in the controller board to accommodate new logical disk sizes, any ST506/412-style drive can be controlled with any standard ST506-type controller. Such drives furnish the controller raw data bits containing both data pulses and timing pulses called clock bits. Data separator circuitry is built into the controller to sort out these two. Unless special encoding techniques are used, this type of interface is generally limited to 5 megabits per second data transfer rates.

Another standard is the enhanced small device interface (ESDI). This interface puts the data separator circuitry in the drive and not the controller. While more expensive to implement, ESDI is potentially much faster than ST506, with the ability to run at 10 to 15 megabits per second.

There has been a trend in recent years to skip the device-level interface entirely and put the controller circuitry right in the disk drive itself. The drive then connects to the computer with a *system-level* interface. Unlike the device-level interface, where information is carried on dedicated lines, system-level interfaces convey information in logical terms. As a result, multiple devices (for example, more than one hard disk drive) can use the same connection in parallel fashion. More intelligence is required to decode requests from the computer (the drive has to decide that the request is for itself and not some other drive on the connection, for instance).

Such system-level interfaces are termed *intelligent*. One

well-known example is the SCSI (small computer system interface). While there was a battle among proponents to refer to the SCSI acronym as "sexy," lack of true standardization has led to the more common reference of "scuzzy."

A SCSI device has circuitry on-board that receives requests for information from the PC, and intelligently handles finding the data, retrieving it, decoding it, and passing it along to the computer on predefined data lines (ideally) common to all SCSI devices. Because the computer does not have to be concerned with the nuts and bolts of operating the peripheral, an SCSI can be a hard disk drive, a tape drive, an optical disk drive, or another peripheral. Such devices are intelligent, so the difference is transparent to the computer system. The SCSI interface has been applied to devices other than storage devices, such as printers and scanners. Unfortunately, manufacturers have had considerable flexibility in terms of what features they include or leave out of their SCSI interface while ostensibly still adhering to the "standard." As a result, there are SCSI interfaces and there are SCSI interfaces, and devices may or may not be compatible among computer systems implementing them.

Disk-Encoding Methods

Controllers and interfaces can be built to accept information more quickly. However, the data transfer rate of a hard disk is necessarily limited by how tightly that information can be packed on the disk. That is, at a given rotational speed, more tightly packed information will be delivered to the read/write heads (and hence the controller) more quickly.

You might compare this to signs placed along the highway. You, the controller, need to be able to read the signs very fast as you pass them. However, since you are limited to 55 miles per hour, no matter how fast you can read, you can only absorb so much information if the signs (each holding 512 bytes of data) are placed 40 feet apart on the highway. But put the signs 20 feet apart, and you will have doubled your ability to pick up information—assuming you can read that fast.

Faster controllers can always be built. So a chief limitation is how information can be placed on the disk and still read by the read/write head. To be read reliably, the bits can be neither spaced too widely apart, nor too closely together. If the bits are too close together, the read/write head doesn't have time to read the bit before the disk surface has moved on to the next bit. If the bits are too far apart, the controller can make errors. Therefore, binary information to be written to disk is *encoded* first, in a way that will minimize these errors.

One basic method of encoding is called *frequency modulation* (FM). With this method, an extra bit called a "clock" bit is recorded just before each data bit. When the disk drive reads back the information from the disk, the presence of the clock bit alerts the controller that a data bit follows. If a flux change is present between two clock bits, the controller interprets that change as a binary 1. If *no* flux change is present, a binary 0 is indicated. Such a system is inherently very reliable, because long strings of binary 0's do not occur together. Neither are two binary 1's ever placed too closely together, because at least one clock bit always separates them. However, two flux changes are needed to record each bit of data, so the FM encoding scheme meant that only 50 percent of a disk could be used for data.

Modified frequency modulation (MFM) records a binary 1 as a flux change, and a 0 as the lack of a flux change within a given period. However, MFM encoding does *not* insert the redundant clock bits between data bits. Instead, an extra flux change (a binary 1) is inserted between consecutive binary 0's to "break" them up. Because so many fewer extra bits are used, MFM is capable of 50 percent higher recording densities than FM. This encoding method is the most common found on hard disks used in IBM PCs and compatibles today.

However, newer schemes are offering promise of even higher densities. In 1986, *Run Length Limited* techniques, in the form of the *2,7 RLL* encoding technology developed by IBM for its mainframes, were applied to microcomputer hard disk controllers. RLL systems convert data through an elaborate coding scheme that allows more information to be recorded in one chunk. Each 8-bit byte received by the controller is translated into a new code pattern 16 bits long. However, only *half* of the possible patterns are used. The other half of the patterns consist of those codes that are most troublesome to record and to read, because they contain long strings of binary 0's. These patterns are never used. The remaining 16-bit code patterns allow from two to a maximum of seven binary 0's between each binary 1. Because of the 2–7-bit spacing, the most common encoding method of this type is called 2,7 RLL (2,9 RLL and other schemes are also used).

Such a system requires twice as many bits to encode the data (16 bits instead of 8 for each 8-bit byte). However, since only the binary 1's cause flux changes, and they are always spaced at least 3 bits apart from each other, the information can be effectively recorded three times as densely. The net result is a recording scheme that is three times as dense as MFM, for 50 percent *more* information per track.

Instead of 17 or 18 sectors, each containing 512 bytes per track, RLL allows from 25 to 27 sectors. A 20-megabyte hard disk can be packed with 30 megabytes of information. Because the hard disk still *rotates* at the same speed, the transfer rate, or rate at which the data is read from the disk, increases proportionately. A typical 5-megabits-per-second rate with MFM encoding is increased by 50 percent to 7.5 megabits under RLL.

More complex encoding schemes have followed. These include *Enhanced Run Length Limited* (ERLL) and *Advanced Run Length Limited* (ARLL). Each manufacturer has tended to apply its own terminology to its specific RLL enhancements. These schemes allow 33 or more sectors of 512 bytes, and a data transfer rate of 9 megabits per second.

All RLL-related encoding schemes require special, complex controllers to encode the data. These controllers don't work with every hard disk, as not all drives are able to handle the increased transfer rate. Controller manufacturers either supply a compatible disk drive or provide a list of tested, recommended models that will work. However, many users of hard disks can upgrade to higher capacity simply by purchasing new controllers for their existing drives. RLL encoding has been applied to hard disks using the ST506/412 interface, and thus can be adapted for a very wide range of devices.

The BIOS and DOS

However, lacking a standard intelligent interface for IBM PCs and compatibles, most hard disks have traditionally used interfaces like ST512 and ST506, which require a greater degree of control by the PC and its operating system. The master control program of the computer, such as MS-DOS or PC-DOS derives its name from *disk operating system* (DOS) because so many of its functions involve disk tasks. DOS also controls writing to your screen, sending files to the printer, and communicating with a modem, but it is known as a disk operating system nonetheless.

Much of the efficiency and resultant limitations on your hard disk drive obtain from the features of DOS. Another factor is the basic input-output system (BIOS) built into the computer in the form of a read-only memory (ROM) chip. The ROM-BIOS contains certain *bootstrap* instructions that tell the computer how to start up when powered on, and also has many *hard*-coded instructions used to access various features of your computer. The BIOS can vary among the different model IBM PCs, as well as between the IBM and compatibles. Because of this, so-called well-behaved software must use *only* DOS features for tasks such as writing to the screen. MS-DOS computers generally operate in the same manner when DOS services are used. To gain speed, programmers frequently call the BIOS routines instead. This is what produces incompatibilities on machines where the BIOS is different.

Having an IBM PC is no guarantee that BIOS will be compatible with later models. For example, the very earliest PCs, as well as some compatibles such as the Compaq and AT&T 6300, don't recognize hard disks. You can determine the release of your IBM PC BIOS with the following BASIC program:

```
10 DEF SEG=&HF000
20 FOR J=&HFFF5 TO &HFFFC
30 PRINT CHR$(PEEK(J));
40 NEXT J
```

The program displays a date. A BIOS earlier than 10/27/82 won't allow booting or accessing a hard disk. Obtain a replacement BIOS from your computer dealer. The only alternative is to boot from a DOS diskette and use a software patch provided by most hard disk manufacturers that will allow reading the hard disk.

Compaq owners can determine their hard disk compatibility by running this program:

```
10 DEF SEG=&HF000:PRINT CHR$(PEEK(&HFFE6))
```

If a letter A or B is displayed, the Compaq is too early a version to run a hard disk. Tandy 1000 owners with the Phoenix Technologies BIOS 1.00 (the BIOS-level message is displayed when the computer is powered on) are in the same fix, and need to get an upgrade from their dealers. For the AT&T 6300, the best way to tell whether the BIOS is version 1.1 or higher (needed for a hard disk) is to read the revision number on the ROM-BIOS chip itself.

Before a hard disk can be used by DOS, it must be *low-level formatted, partitioned,* and *high-level formatted.* The low-level format, often performed by the manufacturer, places basic information on the disk and establishes the interleave factor. A utility program is usually provided with the hard disk to allow the user to reformat the disk to this level later. The process can take from 20 minutes to several hours, depending on the capacity of the disk and the particular formatting program.

Partitioning, done with DOS's FDISK.COM program, sets aside a portion of the disk for the operating systems you will be using. You may partition an entire disk for MS-DOS, or you may divide it among DOS and XENIX, or DOS and CP/M-86. Only rarely will you find a hard disk that has been partitioned for anything other than 100 percent MS-DOS, at least outside the world of AT&T PCs.

The high-level format puts down the information used by DOS to write and read the directory track, and actual data.

No hard disk computer will operate with MS-DOS earlier than version 2.0. Various DOS 2.x and DOS 3.x versions are widely used with hard disks today. A chief advantage of DOS 2.x is that it requires less memory than DOS 3.x. However, it is much less efficient in its use of the disk. When opening a file, DOS will assign sectors to that file in chunks, called *clusters*. With DOS 2.x, the smallest cluster size is 8,192 bytes. DOS 3.x uses 2,048-byte clusters. Therefore, even the smallest, 1-byte file will consume 8,192 bytes on a hard disk formatted under DOS 2.x. A file that is even 1 byte longer than 8,192 will take up *two* clusters, and thus 16,384 bytes of disk space. If your hard disk has a great many small files, such as batch files, or tiny data files, this limitation will prove costly. DOS 3.x's more efficient cluster size can make a major difference in capacity. Disks formatted under earlier versions of DOS can be reformatted using DOS 3.0 or later versions to achieve the smaller cluster size. Just remember to back up all your files first!

This has been a brief introduction to how hard disks work. Now it's time to look at just how they can help you work better, and why you need a hard disk in the first place.

3
Why You Need a Hard Disk

With all the fuss over 80286- and 80386-based computer systems, individuals and organizations may be overlooking their first and most cost-efficient upgrade—to a hard disk. If you are reading this book, you either already have realized this fact or are looking for additional ammunition to help make up your mind, or that of the person who authorizes hard disk purchases in your organization. Here are some powerful reasons why you need a hard disk.

Like many innovations, the most obvious advantages of a hard disk are easy to understand, and alluring: a hard disk offers faster access to greater quantities of on-line storage. However, look a little deeper and you'll find a wealth of productivity-boosting benefits that may not be so apparent at first glance.

- Hard disks allow the manager or worker to maintain a constant workflow. Some jobs call for changing from one application to another only infrequently. A word-processing operator, for example, may load a word-processing program at the beginning of the day and do nothing but text entry and editing for eight hours. Even so, such workers process a variety of files during any given session and, with floppy-disk-based systems, these files are likely to be stored by author, account, date, or some other parameter on a series of separate floppy disks.

Other jobs demand even more frequent disk swapping. A manager or executive may write a memo using word-processing software, switch to a spreadsheet halfway through in order to come up with some figures, then access a database manager, an outliner, or even a communications program in order to check stock quotations through an on-line information service.

In either case, a nightmare of disk swapping is likely to result. With all the software and data a staff member uses on-line on a hard disk at all times, there is no need to stop and hunt for a disk countless times during the day. Data loads from a hard disk six to ten times faster than from a flexible disk.

While the saving may be a few seconds here and a few more there, when those moments are multiplied by 10 or 50 occurrences in a day, the time saved can be substantial. More valuable, however, may be the time the worker doesn't spend shifting gears and breaking up a train of thought. A manager busy analyzing a spreadsheet may decide to look at a second spreadsheet for a quick comparison. With a hard disk that information can be called up in a second or two, viewed, and then the original spreadsheet restored. Using conventional flexible disks, the manager may spend several minutes or decide not to make the comparison at all. Decision support tools are used more efficiently, and *better*, when a hard disk streamlines their operations.

- Hard disks bring entirely *new* capabilities to the desktop. Despite extended memory specifications, most PCs actually in use in the workplace are limited to 640K or less. Moreover, RAM is volatile, and so is suitable only for program files and temporary storage of data files while they are actually being used.

Hard disks, though, can easily function as "virtual," nonvolatile memory for more powerful applications. Windowing environments, for example, allow even more rapid movement back and forth between applications. However, given the

WHY YOU NEED A HARD DISK

memory constraints of 640K, it is often necessary to "swap out" portions of programs and their data to a disk drive when the user switches from one application to another. Hard disk drives make very large programs practical where they are not even possible using flexible disks. There are even utility programs that work in the opposite manner of a RAM disk: they allow the hard disk to function as a slightly slower, but more capacious bank of RAM—as virtual RAM. For programs calling for large quantities of memory, or needing to run sets of programs, each of which takes up large amounts of RAM, you can have available not 640K, or even a megabyte or two of RAM, but 10 or 20 megabytes.

- Hard disks can speed up the operation of programs using overlays, specialized utilities, macro files, or other data. For example, many word-processing programs use format documents, "style sheets," boilerplate paragraphs, and other repetitive material than can be easily kept on a single hard disk ready for instant use. A word-processing department can keep all the different special dictionaries used by their spelling-checker program for trademarks, jargon, proper nouns, in one place.
- Integrated software packages, such as *Symphony, Framework, GEM*, etc., are impractical on floppy-diskette-based systems. Hard disks allow efficient use of such tools. Integrated systems are useful because they allow the user to become comfortable with a single user interface through software that permits sharing of data among several programs. But to be integrated, the package must have all its related modules and their data readily available. How useful is it to be able to import spreadsheet data into your word-processing program if you have to hunt for the spreadsheet disk when that information is needed?
- Computers that are floppy-based are usually underutilized. Since it takes so much time to change from one application or utility to another, such workstations are often used for one or two tasks only, with few, if any, enhancements. If it takes longer to load a tool than to do the job by another means, users will tend to avoid that

tool. For example, the microcomputer thesaurus was introduced in the early 1980s. At that time, it was necessary to exit the word-processing program and load the thesaurus in order to check for synonyms. These steps took longer than would be spent checking a bound paper thesaurus. As a result, few people used a computer version. More recently, versions that can be loaded on a hard disk and accessed through a memory-resident "hot key" have been introduced. Checking for a synonym can be as simple as placing the cursor on a word, pressing the hot key, and waiting two or three seconds while the hard disk synonym list is checked. As this is *much* faster than using a traditional thesaurus, the on-line version has not only replaced the bound volume for many users, it has brought a new tool to users who scarcely bothered to look up synonyms in the past.

Hard disks encourage the use of productivity tools like these, including dictionaries, outliners, schedulers, planners, and on-line phone directories.

- Hard disks allow for a more efficient file structure. A word-processing department may wish to segregate files by author, project, account, or client. This is impractical with conventional flexible disks, which can be completely filled by as few as eight or ten 20-page reports. This forces users to create a *second* disk for a given category, or else create new subcategories. Inevitably, work slows down when workers must decide whether a document is located on disk BUSCH1, BUSCH2, or BUSCH3.

However, separate subdirectories can be created on a hard disk for each type of file. Each subdirectory can hold any size collection of files, up to the size of the hard disk itself. A given disk can keep the equivalent of more than 15,000 double-spaced typed pages (on a 30-megabyte disk).

Other specific programs can benefit from more disk storage. A computer can function as an electronic mailbox or company bulletin board with significant on-line message-storage capabilities using a hard disk drive. Workers can call in from their homes and retrieve documents. Sales staff can file orders. Customers can check on the status of their orders. Messages can be stored and forwarded to workers who are out of town, on vacation, or simply busy. A hard-disk-equipped computer can be the basis of a voice-mail system that users can access from outside with a Touch-tone phone and *no* computer whatsoever.

Accounting functions within small businesses, if handled by a microcomputer, can be more efficient with larger storage capacity readily available. Graphics programs—especially since the new high-resolution video boards promise more professionally oriented computer drafting applications—can access larger image libraries.

In fact, storage of image-intensive information is likely to be a major application for hard disks in the future. More business information than we realize involves images: signatures need to be stored for verification, charts and graphs present numeric information in a way that is more easily grasped and remembered, designs and plans are more easily created and modified with a computer system. Yet, image information requires so much storage space that even high-capacity 1.2 megabyte diskettes are scarcely practical for temporary or long-term storage. Hard disks in the 30–60-megabyte range provide a practical solution.

These are only some of the applications for hard disks in business. Like any relatively new tool, uses are being discovered every day. A hard disk not only makes sense today, but is likely to pay for itself in the future many times over in applications you haven't even thought of.

4
Hard Disk Alternatives

When hard disks for a PC cost $2,000 or more, it was often necessary for a user to cost justify such a major investment. Today, fixed disks are priced at little more than a standard floppy disk drive: $300 and up versus roughly $100. There are, in fact, few "cons" associated with hard disk solutions. Briefly, the major drawbacks, if they can be considered such, are:

- Some users may have to give up a needed disk bay and/or expansion slot to add a hard disk. In some rare instances, a user may not have the space to spare in order to install a hard disk.
- The power supplies in some early PCs and compatibles may not have the capacity to support some power-hungry hard disks. A basic IBM PC has only five slots, which can be quickly filled by a multifunction card, display/printer adapter, expanded memory card, "turbo" speed-up card, and modem card. Even if a slot is available for a hard disk drive or controller, the total drain on the power supply can easily add up to more than 63 watts. The result: the safety mechanism in the power supply trips, powering down the computer.
- Hard disks are a bit more complex to manage and to learn to use properly. Floppy disks are something of an

automatic management system: only small groups of files can fit on each diskette, and the disks themselves can be arranged in a file box by categories. A hard disk, on the other hand, looks like one giant, fast floppy disk to the computer and can quickly become a quagmire into which files vanish, never to be seen again.

This book shows you how to dismiss all of these objections quite easily. However, even with a hard disk purchase simple to justify, it is still important to examine some of the reasons why hard disks are valuable, as we did in the previous chapter. By the same token, looking at some of the alternatives to the hard disk is a useful exercise. Other technologies *can be better* than a hard disk in certain applications, though more frequently they offer capabilities that complement those of the hard disk.

These hard disk "competitors" include RAM, high-capacity floppy disk drives, so-called Bernoulli-effect drives, tape systems, and such exotic fare as bubble memory, optical disk, and *removable* hard disk cartridges.

Hard Disks vs. RAM

RAM, or random-access memory, is nothing more than a collection of impure silicon coated in wafer form on a chip in such a way that the binary 0's and 1's that make up computer information can be stored there. Dynamic RAM must be electrically "refreshed" at millisecond intervals in order to maintain the data for useful periods of time. Some specialized RAM, such as the CMOS (complementary metal oxide semiconductor) variety, requires only a tiny amount of current and thus is suitable for use in battery-powered portables. With some of these, this frugal RAM retains its contents even when the power to the computer is ostensibly switched off. In reality, a small current is supplied to the RAM to keep it refreshed. Truly permanent, static RAM is a more expensive variety that is not widely used in personal computer systems.

For those who have been following the computer scene for some time, the rapid evolution and drastic reduction in price for both RAM and hard disks used in personal computers are somewhat startling. It wasn't too long ago that a hard disk drive with a 3-megabyte capacity was the size of a washing machine, and sold for about $70,000. Today, instead of $23,000 per megabyte, we pay less than $23 per megabyte for disks that are faster, more reliable, and more compact than ever before. A mainframe upgrade of 256K of memory once cost $100,000. Today, a set of nine 256-kilobit chips for a PC cost $40 or less.

When 8-bit machines dominated the personal computer scene, the choice between silicon and magnetic memory was more clear-cut. Your desktop computer probably had 64 kilobyte of RAM (or less) and 100K to 180K of 5¼-inch disk storage per drive. With 8-inch disks, the on-line ante was raised to 250K, 500K, or 1,000K. Those were the only options. RAM was, of course, many times faster than disk "memory," but there was barely enough of it to hold moderate-sized programs in memory at one time. Large programs had to be written in overlays that were swapped in and out of RAM as needed. Your actual working data files were kept on disk and only tiny portions loaded, as necessary, into what remained of RAM.

As 16-bit personal computers began to take over in 1981, and RAM prices plummeted, end users gained a great deal of convenience, and programmers found new flexibility. The next generation of computers could address as much as 640K of RAM at one time. Very large programs could be written and loaded into memory with plenty of room for data. Since access to information in RAM is almost instantaneous, such programs run much more quickly than their 8-bit counterparts that depend more heavily on overlays.

Technology in both the silicon and magnetic memory domains is proceeding at a breathtaking pace. Early personal computers used 16K RAM chips, each storing 16,384 bits of information. A set of eight, costing $100 or more, was required for each bank of 16K memory.

Fortunately, by the time the IBM PC reached significant popularity, 64-kilobit chips were available. A ninth *parity* chip was added to the set of eight to allow storing a parity bit used to check the accuracy of the other eight chips in a 64K bank. Today, 256-kilobit memory chips have become common, at prices of $40 or less for a quarter megabyte of silicon storage. Some computers have sockets that allow installation of either 256-kilobit chips or the newer megabit chips that have been trickling onto the market for some time.

In early 1987 IBM and several other vendors demonstrated high-speed 4-megabit RAM chips with access times of 65 nanoseconds—even faster than the 80-nanosecond access time of the 1-megabit chips used in products like the IBM 3090 mainframes. Meanwhile, Japanese firms worked to perfect 16-megabit chips that pack 40 million circuit elements on a chip less than 9×17 mm in size.

With RAM so cheap—and apparently destined to become cheaper—most 8088-based PCs are sold today with 256K standard, 80286 computers with 512K, and 80386 machines with a megabyte or more as a minimum. This wealth of memory is not too much of a good thing. Believe it or not, for some uses, "temporary" random-access memory may be a viable alternative to "permanent" magnetic memory in the form of removable or fixed disk drives, floppy disks, or magnetic tape. RAM is becoming more generous in personal computers, with 640K almost considered a minimum configuration. "Old" PCs are being equipped with Lotus/Intel Expanded Memory Specification (EMS) cards with extra RAM that can be accessed by applications geared up for it. The 80286-based computers like the IBM PC-AT commonly are equipped with a megabyte or more, even though conventional DOS can handle only 640K of memory. The extra RAM is used by *virtual disk* programs, such as VDISK.SYS, as an "electronic disk." It is also used by special applications and operating systems, such as XENIX.

The PS/2 models 50, 60 and 80 computers and OS/2 operating systems allows even more extensive use of cheap, fast RAM. However, even users of the earliest IBM PCs and compatibles will find that for some uses, RAM can be faster and more effective than even the speediest hard disk.

For example, some applications involve very little disk access. Lotus 1-2-3 spreadsheets must be stored entirely in memory—either conventional RAM or expanded RAM provided through special EMS add-on boards. Once a spreadsheet has been loaded into memory, that file isn't touched again until the user decides to save it and go on to the next task. In such cases, the user would hardly notice whether or not a hard disk was being used to store the worksheet. Workers who use their PCs almost exclusively for spreadsheet applications could conceivably function quite well with a memory-rich computer equipped only with flexible disk drives. Because the Lotus spreadsheets are stored in memory, it is wise to periodically back up the current spreadsheet onto a floppy disk.

On the other side of the coin, a hard disk *can* be a useful accessory in spreadsheet work. Large numbers of worksheets can be stored on the hard disk and accessed quickly without disk swapping. Users who alternate spreadsheet sessions with other applications will appreciate the ability to go back and forth at high speed. It is also faster to back up a spreadsheet to a hard disk, and to retrieve and merge data from hard disk into an existing worksheet.

RAM may also be set aside to simulate a disk drive that is much faster than the fastest hard disk. MS-DOS 3.0 and later versions provide a device driver, VDISK.SYS, that can be used to set up a RAM (virtual) disk automatically each time the system is booted. Add-on memory cards frequently come with software utilities that allow you to set up virtual disks. If expanded or extended memory is used, such memory disks don't even consume any of the 640K of memory allotted for standard DOS applications.

The chief drawbacks to RAM disks are their limited size and their volatility. When the entire "universe" of personal computers is considered, only a tiny percentage are equipped with more than a megabyte of memory; thus, those who can use large RAM disks are an inconsequential minority. Compare this with the estimated 50 percent of users who will have hard disks by 1990. Small RAM disks are limited, since many applications programs are furnished on a number of diskettes. With modern software, all the programs and utilities associated with the application won't fit on a conventional 360K diskette, and certainly won't fit into a 360K RAM disk. A word-processing program, for example, may have one or two disks for all the tasks, plus an additional disk for the spelling checker and dictionaries. Integrated software may be supplied on four or five diskettes, each containing a different portion of the program. Clearly, there are many applications that can't be run from the most common size RAM disk at all.

Some types of virtual disks retain their contents after system resets, alleviating the volatility issue, somewhat. One model battery-operated portable PC can be equipped with 1.2 megabytes of RAM. Two 360K virtual disks may be set up as drives B: and C:. The computer can be rebooted without destroying the contents of these electronic disks. For most users, however, temporary power glitches are likely to be the source of interruptions. Loss of power even for a second will destroy the contents of any virtual disk using dynamic RAM. The only solution here is for battery backup, uninterruptible power sources, or *static* RAM—all fairly expensive alternatives.

Loss of a RAM disk is serious only when data that hasn't been backed up to a magnetic medium is stored on the virtual disk. There is no such risk to running an application from a RAM disk. If RAM becomes corrupted or erased by a glitch in the power line, the application program can quickly be reloaded and the task taken up approximately where the user left off.

Running applications from a RAM disk need be no more complicated than using a magnetic program disk. If your software does require overlays and various utilities that are frequently called from a disk drive, you may copy the application to your RAM disk from the high-capacity disk. This step can be done automatically, through a line or two in an AUTOEXEC.BAT file. The application will run many times faster, and the user can continue to store data on the more secure magnetic media.

With conventional personal computers limited to 512K or 640K of RAM, this method can be a tight memory "fit." The application may use up 192K of RAM. After subtracting the memory taken up by the operating system, there may be only 400K or less left for the RAM disk. With the latest generation computers, such as the IBM PC-AT, this method has been made even more practical by the extended memory available. A megabyte or more can be set aside for a RAM disk. The virtual disk can be invoked through a simple statement in the user's CONFIG.SYS file, and the extra RAM taken advantage of with the /E switch.

The CONFIG.SYS file is a straight ASCII text file, like AUTOEXEC.BAT, to be discussed in more detail later in this book. Normal batch commands cannot be contained in this file, however, and it is accessed by the system on power-up *before* the AUTOEXEC.BAT file is run. There are only a few commands that can be included in the CONFIG.SYS file. The user can tell the system to use alternate device drivers, such as the virtual disk program, VDISK.SYS. A line can be included defining the number of memory buffers to set aside. Those with silicon memory to spare can increase the number of buffers when expecting to run applications that call for many random-access reads and writes. In such cases, the system will check the memory buffer for information before accessing the disk. This is another example of how extra RAM can be used to speed up operations that would otherwise rely on disk accesses. Magnetic memory and silicon memory *do* work together, and should continue to be important tools in the future.

Hard Disks vs. High-Capacity Diskettes

With the PC-AT, personal computer users found themselves faced with a new flexible diskette option: the 1.2 megabyte high-capacity diskette. At about the same time, Eastman Kodak Company introduced a similar technology offering 3.3 megabytes of unformatted capacity, and a year later, a 6.6-megabyte diskette.

All these high-capacity diskettes use floppies that look a great deal like conventional 5¼-inch diskettes, but which actually are quite different. They are coated with a magnetic material capable of storing much more information than ordinary disks, because of its "high coercivity." This property is commonly rated in *oersteds* (abbreviated Oe). High-capacity diskettes have 600 Oe coatings, compared to the roughly 300 Oe coatings on conventional diskettes. In addition, disks like the Kodak media have factory-encoded *servo* information, allowing the special disk drives needed to read them to stay reliably within the much narrower tracks, spaced 192 tracks per inch, compared to the 48 tracks per inch (tpi) on conventional diskettes.

The Kodak intelligent 12-megabyte disk drive increases the track count again to 333 tpi, and boosts capacity further by increasing the number of sectors within each track. Its servomechanism is even more sophisticated, and uses a precise voice-coil motor to position the carriage.

Many of the problems associated with hard disk drives are eliminated with any of the high-capacity drives. Head crashes, for example, don't occur with this type of drive. Permanently installed fixed disk drives are difficult to protect from unauthorized use and complicate sharing of information. This is not a problem with high-capacity drives.

High-capacity disks and their drives bear a greater resemblance to conventional floppy disks both in terms of convenience of transport, and in the techniques used to read and write data. Like the standard disk drive, the read/write heads in the drives come into actual contact with the media. A pair of heads press gently against opposite sides of the diskette, maintaining the necessary contact. A contact recording/reading system eliminates the worry of deadly head crashes. Dirt and grime can make any diskette unreadable, but elaborate sealing mechanisms such as those found in hard disks are not necessary.

High-capacity diskettes offer some of the advantages of hard disks in terms of capacity and improved data transfer speed. None are as fast as hard disks, however. This is true because in most cases (the Kodak 12-megabyte drive is an exception) the disk drive comes to a halt in between accesses. When the user accesses data again, the disk drive must wait for the motor to bring the rotational speed of the diskette up to the correct pace before the read can begin.

Also, none of these diskettes have a capacity to match the largest of the fixed disk drives. In addition, because the head actually contacts the disk surface, high-capacity diskettes can wear out.

Hard Disks vs. Optical Disks

Optical disks record data by writing a series of pits with a laser on a disk-shaped medium. When a laser is later used to read these pits, the original information can be retrieved. Capacity is greater because the precision of the laser allows burning pits much closer together than is possible with magnetic media. (One type of optical disk has not 333 tracks per inch of disk radius, but 14 *thousand.* Total capacity for this 14-inch optical disk is 6,800 megabytes!)

Optical disk drives are not currently a competitor with the average hard disk, because the variety that can be written to as well as read costs a minimum of ten to twenty times the price of the average hard disk drive. Even read-only optical disks with no capability for the user to write data onto them cost more than some of the lowest-priced hard disk drives.

However, keep in mind the washing-machine-sized, $70,000 hard disk drives that now fit in the palm of your hand and cost $400 or less. Optical disk technology is in its infancy. Any user of a very large hard disk—in the 100-megabyte and up range—should at least consider how optical disks will certainly affect him or her in the future.

Because the technology is so new, optical disks are something of a cure in search of a suitable disease. As optical disk technology matures over the next several years, developing applications for this storage medium will become as important as refining the technology itself. However, there are already a wealth of uses and potential uses shaping up for each of the three current categories of optical disk media—read-only, write-once, read mostly (WORM), and fully erasable optical disks.

The so-called compact disk read-only memory (CD-ROMs) are ROMS only in the sense that the end user may not write to them. All the information contained in a CD-ROM is written during fabrication in much the same manner as compact disk audio recordings. This type of optical disk is suited for publishing a large database of information, especially those that do not change very frequently. Users may look up information just as they would with an on-line database, or a large collection of printed material, but without incurring connect-time charges. The CD-ROM also puts the power of the computer to use, quickly searching for and accessing any given piece of information from within the vast store that can be housed on a single disk.

For example, one database available on CD-ROM includes financial information for more than 10,000 public companies, based on reports filed with the U.S. Securities and Exchange commission. A text-only version of Grolier's Academic American encyclopedia is also available in this format. Reference works of this type can be updated annually or semiannually, and the user supplied with a new version at intervals.

In the future, attorneys may be able to purchase entire law libraries on optical disks. Professionals may subscribe to *all* the journals in their field through a single optical disk joint-publishing effort. Sophisticated software—which could incorporate artificial intelligence—could be used to scan through each current set of issues to find specific articles of interest to the subscriber.

Because of the cost involved in preparing the "master" disk, and the comparative low cost of each subsequent copy, such publishing today is most practical either where a large number of copies can be sold, or where the information is valuable enough that individual subscribers are willing to pay their proportionate cost of a smaller edition.

The write-once, read mostly (WORM) optical disk is a second technology that will see widespread applications. Optical disk is particularly well suited to image information simply because its prodigious capacity matches the huge amount of information available in a typical image. Much of the data we must deal with originates in hard-copy document form: signatures, graphs, charts, seals, photographs, and additional valuable image information. While a standard 80-character × 25-line computer screen can contain, at the most, 2,000 characters of data, a single 8½ x 11-inch sheet of paper, scanned at 200 dots per inch, contains 3.7 *million* bits of data.

As the need to store and electronically manipulate image information grows, the very large storage capacities offered by optical disk technology become more interesting. WORM optical disks can be useful for applications where an original database or set of image information must be stored in a compact form, yet still be available for fast access.

There are also many applications in fields such as graphic arts. Users may want to store color separations, or images of entire digitized pages, on such optical disks for reprinting, or as part of a "morgue" of information and images that may be reused in whole or part at some later date. The government wants to digitize training manuals. Hospitals want to store digital examinations from CAT scanners and magnetic resonance imaging, and manufacturers of weapon systems, power plants, and other complex products need to store and retrieve millions of engineering drawings.

With optical disks in an automated disk library—a "jukebox" where the cartridge can be retrieved automatically like a mass-storage system—a whole host of applications becomes feasible. These large files are now stored in tape libraries. The most obvious examples come from many government applications where hundreds of forms are required: the Internal Revenue Service, the Securities and Exchange Commission, and the U.S. Patent Office.

The third form of optical disk technology—fully erasable optical disks—has already been demonstrated in prototype form. The pioneer in erasable optical disks is Verbatim Corporation. In 1985 Verbatim demonstrated an experimental thermo-magneto-optics (TMO) disk at the National Computer Conference.

These efforts have concentrated on developing a writing process that involves a reversible physical change in the storage medium. From a user's standpoint, the attributes of this technology translate into the advantages of media removability and interchangeability, complete write-read capabilities, random access to the data, and archivability of the data.

Erasable optical disks have broad applications for high-density, high-activity storage with increased reliability. For many users, they will replace hard disks by offering high-storage capacity at a lower media cost, and without the risk of loss of data due to head crashes and other catastrophes.

In addition to serving as a storage medium for on-line, frequently updated material, erasable optical disks can also be used for any application where CD-ROM or WORM technology is likely to be used. For example, if, in the future, you receive a complete library of data in optical disk form, you may be able to update that library yourself, make notes, add articles from other sources, and perform other additions that will make the information more useful to you. With erasable media, graphic arts houses will not only be able to store their color separations on optical disk, but provide corrections and changes on the same media. Your photofinisher may someday capture image information from your snapshots, and then keep the data on file permanently, so that if you want a new enlargement, you may order one without bothering to locate the negative.

Hard Disks vs. Removable Hard Disks

Removable hard disks are much like the fixed disk, except that the hard disk media is contained in a carrier that can be removed from the disk drive when desired. These drives suffer the same sensitivity to dust and dirt that a sealed hard disk is susceptible to. The drive is sealed only after the cartridge has been inserted, and a valiant attempt is made to evacuate and/ or filter the dirty air. Such measures are not foolproof, however, and hard disk cartridge drives have had something of a reputation for unreliability in the past.

Such media could also be damaged by dropping the precision cartridge a few inches. Given the development of less finicky removable media, hard disk cartridges are not used much today. This technology should not be confused with some specialized hard disks that allow removal of the entire drive from its bay or slot, nor should it be confused with external hard disks which are simply hard disks mounted in their own box with a separate power supply and connected to the PC with a cable.

Hard Disks vs. Tape Cartridge Storage

Tape cartridge systems are widely used as a *backup* medium for hard disks, rather than as primary storage media themselves. The reason for this is that, for the most part, tape systems store an *image-oriented* rather than a *file-oriented* set of data. That is, the drive makes an exact bit-by-bit image copy of the hard disk onto tape. The information can only be retrieved by restoring that image to the hard disk.

More recently, tape systems that store information addressable by *files* have become available. These come with software that allows individual files to be restored rather than the entire disk. Some even allow DOS to treat the tape as if it were a standard disk drive, and allow programs to be run directly from the tape. Even so, tape is still a serial medium; it is necessary to run a tape all the way to the end to access a file at that position on the tape. File-addressable tape systems will be most useful for those who occasionally need to access an individual file from their archive, rather than for those who need constant, convenient storage and retrieval of information.

Hard Disks vs. Bernoulli-Effect Drives

There are several add-on devices that take advantage of a fluid dynamics principle discovered by Daniel Bernoulli in the 1700s. They all use 8-inch or smaller flexible media, like floppy disks, but use a noncontact recording/reading technique that allows high capacities, rivaling those of a hard disk.

The so-called Bernoulli effect is produced when the flexible disk spins at high speeds. Airflow holds the spinning disk at a stable and frictionless 10 microinches from the aerodynamically shaped head. Drives using this technology are capable of storing 20 megabytes or more of information.

The removable media are not expensive to buy on a per-megabyte basis. However, access is slower than for hard disks, and in most cases a special card is required to allow the PC to boot from the drive. The original Bernoulli drives were large and somewhat cumbersome (as you might expect from any drive using 8-inch media). More recently, other manufacturers have introduced smaller drives using reduced-size, less expensive media. If the slower access speed is acceptable, these drives present an alternative to hard disks for applications where security is a major consideration, since the media can be locked up for protection. Those with large databases can swap media in and out, as required.

However, for most, a hard disk is the better option. For databases of 60 megabytes or less, sufficient hard disk capacity can be installed to allow you to keep *all* the information online, with no media swapping necessary. The hard disk allows faster access to that information and provides a security aspect of its own: no one can run off with your database because you forgot to lock it up properly.

Hard Disks vs. Bubble Memory

Magnetic bubble memory made quite a splash a few years ago because it was nonvolatile, sufficiently fast, and, at that time, could be purchased at not too great a cost when compared to conventional RAM or hard disks. Now, hard disks and RAM have plummeted in price, while bubble memory, if you can find it, remains expensive by comparison.

Research breakthroughs may bring down the cost of bubble memory cards in the future. At present, however, this option is most suitable only for use in hostile environments where hard disk data could be damaged by vibration or other hazards.

5
Hard Disk Options

One of the reasons a book like this one is needed is that once a user has decided that a hard disk will indeed provide the solutions he or she is looking for, there are still dozens of options to consider. This chapter will help you weigh the alternatives and decide which type of hard disk is best for you. We'll cover the advantages and disadvantages of hard disks mounted in disk drive bays, on internal cards, and externally. Because hardware changes so quickly, discussions of specific brands of drives and computers will be minimized. Instead, the information in this chapter can be used to select your hard disk no matter what offerings are on the market at the time you are ready to make a decision.

Bay-Mounted Hard Disks

Most of the first hard disks sold for IBM PCs and compatibles were designed to fit in one of the mounting bays originally occupied by a floppy disk drive, as a replacement for that floppy disk. Early IBM PC-XTs, for example, were equipped with one *full-height* (roughly 4 inches tall) floppy disk drive, and one full-height 10-megabyte hard disk drive. In this configuration, users have the use of only one floppy disk, of course. For the most part, the loss has limited impact, since the hard disk is used for most data and program storage. For many users, the single floppy disk drive is used only to dump data for backup or exchange, or to load programs supplied on diskette to the hard disk. When a computer is configured with only one floppy disk drive, DOS will automatically treat that one *physical* drive as two *logical* drives.

For example, if you are copying from one disk to another, you may specify COPY A:*.* B: just as if there were two disk drives installed. DOS will display the message INSERT DISKETTE FOR DRIVE A: or INSERT DISKETTE FOR DRIVE B: at the appropriate times during the copy process. This may be mildly confusing for some, and can lead to errors if the wrong diskette is inserted at the wrong time, but it is generally a workable solution. DRIVER.SYS, provided with DOS 3.2 and later versions, allows you to specify even *more* logical identifiers for a single disk drive. An 80286-based computer with only one 1.2 megabyte drive can be set up so that drive D: (still the 1.2 meg drive) is always considered to be a standard 360K drive.

Those with lots of memory and DOS 3.2 or later can also benefit from XCOPY, an extended copy command that optimizes single-drive copies by loading as many files into memory as possible before asking for the disk swap. However, those who do a great deal of copying from one diskette to another, or who like to store files to a "scratch" diskette in A: and to a "backup" diskette in B: will miss having a second disk drive.

Fortunately, drive manufacturers have greatly miniaturized the components needed to build both flexible and hard disk drives. So-called half-height drives are available for each type of drive and have become something of a standard for more recently designed PCs and compatibles. When half-height drives are used, *two* floppy disk drives can be mounted in one bay of a PC, PC-XT, or compatible, leaving the other bay free for a full-height hard disk, or two half-height hard disks. Some computers have more than two bays, providing room for even more flexible drive configurations. However, some have fewer. Various models of the Tandy 1000, for example, were designed with a compact footprint and only enough room for two bay-mounted half-height drives—either a half-height floppy and a half-height hard disk, or two floppy disk drives.

HARD DISK OPTIONS

Bay-mounted hard disks can be mounted in PCs in a number of ways, depending on the computer itself. While hard disk cards have received the bulk of the attention in recent months, the traditional internally mounted hard disk has some advantages.

First, full- and half-height bay-mounted hard disks are available in higher capacities than the run-of-the-mill hard disk card, and at lower cost. A 40-megabyte hard disk card may cost twice as much as a bay-mounted hard disk of the same capacity, because of the special miniaturization techniques that must be used. Go much beyond 60 megabytes, and you're in totally foreign territory for the hard disk card. Yet bay-mounted units of 100 megabytes or more have been available for years.

Several bay-mounted hard disks can be put in one computer and operated from a single controller card. Multiple hard disk cards can also be operated from a single controller, but each card you add consumes another slot. In computers with limited slot space, this can be a serious constraint.

The conventional hard disk is less sensitive to vibration and movement of the computer because, even in half-height configuration, the drive can be installed in a heftier, better-isolated mount. Hard disk cards, on the other hand, have to be "ruggedized" to protect their sensitive surfaces from possible damage when the computer is moved or accidentally bumped. Neither type drive is particularly fragile or unreliable, but if your computer is likely to be moved frequently or subject to unexpected shocks (which would make them not entirely unexpected), consider a bay-mounted hard disk.

Finally, some prefer a bay-mount unit because almost all of them have a front-mounted LED that shows when the drive is operating. Hard disk cards may put a blinking character on your screen or offer an add-on LED that you mount yourself. Of you may just have to rely on the sound of the hard disk card as an indicator.

In summary, don't write off the traditional hard disk simply because it is "older" technology than hard disk cards. Such disk drives will continue to be improved in the future, and there are some solid reasons why they are better for many applications.

Hard Disk Cards

In contrast to the bay-mounted hard disk, which requires a separate controller card and hard disk, the hard disk card is an all-in-one unit that can provide 10 or 20 megabytes of storage—or more—on a single card that may occupy only a slot or two in the computer. Installation is often a simple, plug-in procedure. What could be simpler?

Hard disk cards can actually occupy "zero" slots. Some hard disk controllers have been built that can also control the system's floppy disks. So, the floppy disk controller can be removed and replaced with a card that can handle the floppy disks, the hard disks, and include the hard disk itself—with no additional slots occupied.

More common are cards that take up one slot, a slot and a half (allowing half-size cards such as modems to be used in the "half" slot), or even more. Despite this penalty in expansion slots, hard disk cards have become one of the fastest-growing mass-storage options on the market.

Convenience is one powerful motivator. As we've seen, conventional hard disks are more complicated to install. The user has to remove one of the computer's flexible disk drives, or hook up a separate external housing which, in some cases, could be an "expansion unit" as large as the PC's system unit. Routing power and data cables can be tricky, and the user sometimes has to install a delicate ROM chip to allow the computer to recognize the new drive. If the hard disk replaces a flexible disk, the user has to reset DIP switches on the system board to account for the new configuration and, moreover, lacks the convenience and security of having two floppy drives.

Today, the upgrade to hard disk drive can be as simple as sliding the cover off the PC and slipping the hard disk card into an empty slot. In most cases, only a single slot will be filled by the card. Users with computers such as the IBM PC-XT with a built-in hard disk can *add* a second hard disk without taking up any additional slots. The existing hard disk controller card is removed and replaced with the card, and the cable from the older hard disk drive is plugged into the new controller.

Most users have had the opportunity to plug in a memory card, modem board, or other accessory, and will be very comfortable with installing their own hard disk cards. In fact, some users transport these cards between computers occasionally as a way of "relocating" their workstation to another department, or taking their data home for working on weekends, or efficiently moving large quantities of data from one computer to another. Because of the time needed to disconnect all the cables and take the cover off the PC, this method isn't recommended as an everyday practice, but certainly it is more convenient than if the hard disk were a bay-mounted unit.

In an age of fast-moving computer technology, plug-in hard disk cards are one way to bring older, flexible-disk-based systems up to the performance standards users are demanding today. The hard disk on a plug-in card, considered a technical marvel when these devices debuted in 10-MB form, now can be purchased in 20- to 30-megabyte sizes—and up. Today, users who appreciate the convenience of simply plugging as much mass storage as they need into a vacant slot wonder if there is any limit on the capacity of hard disk cards.

In truth, current hardware and software limitations on hard disk card capacity are real, but far from insurmountable. First, we need to consider the physical size of the hard disk card itself. The development of 3½-inch half-height hard disk drives, special encoding techniques like 2,7 RLL that boost the capacity of a 20-megabyte drive to 30 megabytes, and electronic innovations like surface-mount technology have allowed more flexible configuration of hard disk drives in PCs.

The capacity of hard disk cards is usually increased by adding platters, which makes the card thicker. Since users generally prefer hard disk cards that occupy a single slot, spacing can be especially critical in computers like the IBM PC-XT and others with narrower intervals between slots. So one limitation on the storage possible with these drives is the ingenuity of the manufacturer in using techniques such as very compact voice-coil motor head positioning to allow compact, high-density drives.

While the manufacturers' goal is to provide as much hard disk card storage as possible per slot occupied in the PC, end users today also have the option of expanding their capacity by plugging additional cards into free slots. As a result, the amount of internal storage is also limited by the number of slots available. Users can add two new hard disks as drives C: and D:, but only if free slots are available.

Many PCs today have extra slots available. Others can be configured with multifunction cards containing memory, extended memory, parallel and serial ports, and even graphics/display circuitry that free up slots formerly occupied by multiple cards. By plugging two 30-MB hard disk cards into these free slots, a worker with heavy storage requirements could custom build a PC with 60 MB of hard disk capacity in a few minutes. (The most advanced cards can be plugged in with no need for power cables or other special installation procedures.)

Even basic PCs with the standard 63-watt power supply can often handle the extra (approximately 14-watt) power demands of a hard disk card. However, as the number of accessories, including flexible disks, add-on cards, and more hard disk drives, increases, users will want to consider using a larger 135-watt or 195-watt supply.

External Hard Disks

External hard disks are simply bay-mounted hard disk units that are installed in separate housings with their own power supplies. Most frequently, the disk controller card must still be positioned in one of the system unit's expansion slots.

One key advantage to an external hard disk is that a large quantity of storage can be fit into the cabinet, with no loss of internal bay space. Two or more full-height hard disks can be accommodated, providing 100, 240, or more megabytes of capacity. The external drive is equipped with its own power supply, putting little or no additional strain on the system unit's supply.

Some manufacturers use a disk controller within the external drive, and interface to the computer through an auxiliary card and cable. Several computers can be equipped with these interfaces, allowing the external drive to be easily unplugged and moved from computer to computer.

On the negative side, external drives have traditionally been more expensive than internal drives with the same capacity. The usual penalty is about $200 or more, to account for the cabinet and additional hardware. Moreover, an external drive is obviously more prone to theft and accidental damage, and can require more desk space (unless it is tucked out of sight).

Today, external hard disks are a somewhat specialized product, used primarily for those who need the maximum possible hard disk capacity and who are willing to pay a cost premium.

Hard Disk Capacity: Where Is the Ceiling?

The versions of MS-DOS that most of us use provide an upward limitation on the size of hard disk that can be considered as a single volume, currently 32 megabytes. The reason for this is that DOS keeps track of disk storage by clusters. Each cluster, or group of sectors, on the disk is assigned to individual files through what is called the *file allocation table,* or FAT. Because this "road map" is so essential, DOS keeps two copies of the FAT on the disk to preserve integrity.

With the FAT arranged in this way, DOS is able to use the available disk space very flexibly. If all disk sectors in a file had to be arranged together *(contiguously),* as files were killed and created, DOS would need to try and find a continuous space on the disk into which a new file would fit. Since files can become larger, DOS would need to know, in advance, how large a contiguous space a file would require.

Instead, using the FAT, DOS is able to fit bits and pieces of a file into any available space, without regard to the physical location on the disk. Clusters can be assigned dynamically, as required, for a given file. Of course, DOS still attempts to write a file as continuously as possible, because *unfragmented* files can be retrieved faster. However, preventing fragmentation entirely would make a hard disk almost unusable without periodic time-consuming "housekeeping." It's more efficient to allow such storage, even though the arrangement itself causes the need for periodically "cleaning up" a heavily fragmented disk file structure.

The original specification for the FAT used a 12-bit number to track the allocation of each available cluster of sectors. As a result, there could be only 4,096 unique cluster numbers, with some of these reserved for DOS, leaving 4,078 that could actually be used to allocate clusters. As described in chapter 2, clusters are created in a fixed size, usually 2,048 bytes for a hard disk formatted under DOS 3.x, and later versions, and 8,192 bytes under earlier versions of DOS. Multiplying 4,078 unique cluster addresses by an 8,192-byte cluster size yields a maximum possible addressable disk capacity of 33,406,976 bytes, or roughly 32 megabytes.

DOS 3.x reduced the cluster size to 2,048, which logically would also quarter the maximum addressable capacity of the disk. However, at the same time, the FAT entry size was modified to support either a 12-bit *or* a 16-bit number, so the maximum unique clusters can now be 65,536 (65,518 usable to allocate clusters), for a *potential* upper limit of 134,180,864 bytes.

However, releases of DOS at this writing don't take full advantage of this, allowing just 16,384 FAT entries, for a maximum single volume of—you guessed it—32 megabytes. Still, unless a user has an applications program that limits data file size to the size of the hard disk, and that user also has a single data file approaching 32 megabytes in size, this software limitation is not likely to be much more than an annoyance.

Two 32-MB or smaller hard disks can easily be used in a single system under different drive names. The worker may want to store all applications programs on one hard disk, and keep the second free for data files. Even when hard disk cards exceed 32 MB, the user is free to partition them into smaller logical drives.

Patches to existing DOS versions, and future versions of DOS, make this restriction even less of an annoyance. Manufacturers of hard disks and hard disk cards provide software that allows the computer to logically treat a larger drive as a single volume, even though DOS still handles the hard disk as if it were two units.

Specific Computer Configurations

All three types of hard disks—internal bay mount, hard disk card, and external—can generally be installed in any given IBM PC or compatible computer. However, there are some considerations you should take into account, as each type of computer has limitations and advantages with respect to the hard disk type you choose. We'll look at IBM PCs, PC-XTs, 80286 and 80386 computers like the PC-AT and PS/2, as well as compatibles.

IBM PCs and IBM PCs with Expansion Unit

The original, now discontinued IBM PC has five expansion slots for cards such as monitor/printer adapter, multifunction cards, network cards, and the separate hard disk controller card needed with all bay-mounted hard disks. With two bays, the PC has room for only one full-height flexible disk and one full-height hard disk, or some combination of one to four half-height drives.

Because of the limited number of slots, some users found themselves running out of places to plug in their hard disk controller. The original PC, with its 63-watt power supply, frequently cannot provide adequate power for a full complement of internally mounted hard and flexible disk drives and add-on cards. IBM made available an expansion unit, the same size and shape as the system unit, but with additional slots and a power supply. A cable connects the expansion unit with the system unit. This is a clumsy, expensive, and rarely used solution to the expansion problems of the average user.

Instead, new, higher capacity power supplies costing $100 or less can be dropped in to replace the existing PC supply, and cards that combine many functions can free up additional slots. For example, cards with memory, serial and parallel ports, clock, as well as monochrome and color graphics display capabilities are available. Half-height drives provide the equivalent of the bay space found in an expansion unit. There is little reason for a user to consider an expansion unit today.

As mentioned in chapter 1, very early model PCs had a ROM-BIOS that would not recognize hard disks. Users with those computers should consider upgrading their ROM to get the most use from a hard disk drive.

IBM PC-XTs

IBM PC-XT models, except for the IBM PC-XT-286, share the configuration of the ordinary PC, except that the PC-XT has eight expansion slots, six full-length slots spaced more closely together than in a PC, and two half-size slots located behind the left-hand disk drive bay. In addition, the PC-XT comes standard with a 135-watt power supply. Therefore, bay-mounted hard disks are less likely to overload the power supply, and most users will have a slot or two to spare for the hard disk controller card.

Originally, the PC-XT designation indicated a computer with a single full-height IBM-installed floppy disk, and a full-height IBM-installed 10-megabyte hard disk. Eventually, IBM made available PC-XTs with one or two (or *no*) flexible disks and, if desired, no hard disk. The PC-XT gradually replaced the basic PC as the bottom-of-the-line IBM PC model.

Accordingly, many users in recent years purchased PC-XT models with floppy disk drives only, and added their own lower-cost hard disks. Most other considerations in buying and installing a bay-mounted hard disk in a PC-XT are the same as for a basic PC, except that all PC-XT models have a ROM-BIOS compatible with hard disk operation.

Because of the narrower spacing between the expansion slots on the PC-XT, hard disk cards that take up only a single slot in the PC or a compatible may intrude on an additional slot in the XT. Some manufacturers design their hard disk cards so that a bit of the "overhang" extends on *both* sides of the card. By moving the XT's internal speaker to an alternate location, and putting the hard disk card in the leftmost slot, an extra-wide card can be installed without taking up a valuable expansion slot.

Compatible Computers

The term compatible, when applied to computer systems, is a relative term. Even within the IBM line, there are many instances of hardware and software operating properly with one configuration, but not another. The ill-fated IBM PC*jr* is one example of the "true blue" IBM computer using the same Intel 8088 microprocessor as the standard PC and PC-XT, but which couldn't run the same software because of a slightly different ROM-BIOS and video display management scheme.

Of course, it is true that "well-behaved" software that accesses the hardware only through DOS (and not directly) should operate on *any* compatible PC. But, given the speed penalties imposed by DOS services for such tasks as writing to the screen, many software authors have used faster, hardware-dependent techniques that have made computers like the PC*jr* and non-IBM PCs less compatible. Only a few years ago, such systems were frequently measured in terms of IBM compatibility, using "difficult" programs like Microsoft's *Flight Simulator* as a test. Since the chief source of incompatibility is found in differences between the ROM-BIOS, several third-party firms invested a considerable amount of programmer effort in independently developing their own BIOS routines that closely mimic the IBM ROM without duplicating the copyrighted code. All software calls to these BIOS routines generally produce the same results as calls to the IBM BIOS, even though the code itself is (supposedly) different. The efforts have been so successful that nearly all clones and compatibles today are as close to 100 percent IBM compatible from a software standpoint as any system is likely to get. Nearly all software will run on any PC, as long as the other hardware specifications called for (proper display adapter, disk drives, etc.) are followed.

Hardware compatibility, particularly as it applies to hard disk users, is another matter. Minor differences such as layout of the keyboard have little consequence to those seeking to expand their mass-storage capabilities. Of greater import are the number and size of expansion slots available, and the power supply built into the compatible.

Believe it or not, some compatibles have power supplies that are even *smaller* than those built into the stock IBM PC. Because these computers are not necessarily laid out internally like the IBM products, upgraded power supplies may not be readily available.

Other incompatibilities may develop in terms of the size and number of expansion slots. PC compatibles have as few as three expansion slots, and some computers accept only 10-inch cards, as opposed to the full-size 13-inch cards used for most hard disk controllers and hard disk cards.

Small footprint PCs may have only a single disk drive bay with two half-height floppy disks, reducing mounting options further. If you are purchasing a compatible computer specifically to upgrade to hard disk storage, be sure and check out these considerations. The manufacturer may supply a hard disk option; if so, this may be your best choice to ensure that the hardware all works together. However, if everything else checks out, hard disks from third parties can be installed in most compatibles fairly easily.

80286, 80386, and Beyond

The IBM PC-AT ushered in a new era of advanced PCs, with expanded options in many areas, including the hard disk storage arena. More recently, computers based on the 80386 microprocessor have loomed large in many business users' computer planning.

Faster computers can accept and process data at a faster rate, calling for faster and larger hard disk drives. Instead of the 85 ms access time typical of PC-XT-era computers, the latest generation can use speedier hard disk drives with sub-40 ms access speeds. Certainly, no one who has invested in an 80286 or 80386 computer will want to slow down their system performance by shackling their machine to a sluggish hard disk.

The first of this breed, the PC-AT, brought several changes to the PC hard disk world other than speed. The

PC-AT and its clones generally incorporate space for additional bay-mounted disk drives, making it easier to install pairs of 30- or 40-megabyte drives for 60 to 80 megabytes of internal storage. The AT upped the minumum configuration for a hard-disk-based computer to 20 megabytes.

ATs also incorporated a built-in hard disk controller, which could explicitly operate 15 different types of hard disk arrangements. Finally, the AT introduced the built-in PC key lock, which brought a needed measure of security to users with a heavy investment in the data stored on their hard disks.

Those looking for optimum performance as well as largest capacity should consider the extra investment in an 80286 or 80386 computer such as the PS/2.

6
Tailoring Mass Storage to the Job at Hand

We've covered in detail the available hard disk options except for one: what capacity do you need for your specific application? A few years ago, microcomputer users had few options in planning their mass-storage requirements. If they were lucky, they could choose between single-sided and double-sided flexible disk drives. Many computers were available with one or the other, but seldom was there a choice for the end user.

Since 1983, when the hard disk drive began to see widespread use, it has become a standard offering from many manufacturers of desktop and portable microcomputers. However, in the early days choices were severely limited. You could take the 10-megabyte hard disk offered by the manufacturer, or, perhaps, shop around and find higher-capacity hard disks available from third-party sources.

Today, the choices have proliferated. Ten to 60 megabytes of internal hard disk storage are offered by most IBM PC and compatible manufacturers. The number of "aftermarket" sources for fixed disk drives, removable cartridge drives, streaming tape systems, and other mass-storage alternatives has grown.

The choices don't stop there. Microcomputers can be linked through local area networks (LANs) to file servers with their own mass-storage capabilities. In fact, some networks allow personal computers to "boot up" through the file server so that a PC-based workstation can function without any dedicated mass storage at all.

In addition to fixed disks, which cannot be removed from the computer without taking the cover off, users also can choose from options such as those described in chapter 4. While none of the alternative mass-storage technologies currently provide all the advantages of an internal hard disk, some of them offer additional benefits that can be used in tandem. For example, in an office, and external storage device with removable media can provide a convenient way of backing up data from one or serveral PCs.

Here are some criteria you can use in estimating your own mass-storage needs.

Will the Micros Stand Alone?

Obviously, any microcomputer used outside a network will require mass storage of its own. But how isolated will the workstations be, in terms of the data and programs that they will use? PCs used by managers in their own offices for decision-making purposes are usually dedicated to that manager's use alone. The manager will want to keep all the applications software and data available and easy to access, without a lot of disk swapping. In such cases, a standard 5¼- or 3½-inch disk drive or two will probably not do the job. The manager's very valuable time shouldn't be wasted hunting for disks and spending a minute or two moving from one application to another.

Instead, it would be desirable to have a hard disk available to streamline data and program access. Ten-megabyte disk drives, fast becoming an extinct species, are probably too skimpy in capacity for any but the occasional business user. A company with an inventory of older IBM PC-XT models or other computers with 10-megabyte drives would probably be wise to rotate these workstations to users who are just moving up to a PC, or those with limited need for large amounts of data.

A small Lotus 1-2-3 worksheet, for example, can easily consume 20K, and word-processing programs that store text in special formats, such as *DisplayWrite 3* and *4*, will eat up 30–50K per file. Assuming that a third of a 10-MB disk is allocated to software, adding one or two files per day will deplete all available data storage space in six to nine months. So, any 10-MB hard disk drives in an organization are best assigned to users with more modest requirements.

In the stand-alone situation described, even a 20-megabyte drive is likely to be rapidly filled. If the user is loaded down with very large applications programs, or happens to be using a special operating system (XENIX, for example, requires 7 MB just for the operating system files), 30 to 40 megabytes is more reasonable.

Before going to the extra expense of installing such a massive hard disk drive, consider whether some of the information can be archived to tape or floppy disks. High-capacity diskettes, capable of storing 1.2 MB and up, reduce the inconvenience of transferring large quantities of information to removable media. If a file is accessed once a quarter, it may be a candidate for off-line storage. When only information needed for day-to-day operation is kept on the hard disk, security is improved and the user's file structure is leaner and easier to access and maintain.

Consider also that most users don't take proper security precautions with a hard disk and are forced to leave their valuable data exposed when they leave their desks for a break or at the end of the day. In industries where security is very tight, or in businesses where knowledge workers frequently move from one workstation to another, it might make sense to have a high-capacity floppy disk drive installed in each PC. Then, applications programs, utilities, and other less-sensitive files would be stored in the hard disk to provide fast booting, near-instant loading of programs, and other hard disk benefits. The sensitive data files would be stored only on the floppy disks, which could be removed from the computer and locked in a safe for protection. No other user of that workstation would have access to those files without physically locating the diskettes.

You can estimate the mass-storage requirements of a "stand-alone" user fairly easily by looking at the number of applications that the worker uses and the size of the data files that the manager or others in similar positions already are accessing.

Will the Workstation Be Part of a Network?

The file server in a network will have large quantities of memory storage available. There will usually be passwords and other protection schemes that restrict access. In such cases, neither local capacity nor local security may be much of a concern. In fact, as mentioned, some workstations may not have any internal mass data storage at all.

Even so, there are good reasons why networked PCs should also include mass storage. An executive may want to download some information to take home or to an out-of-town business meeting. The worker may also wish to use applications programs not available on the network for some specialized task. Again, since even the fastest networks cause some delays and can have degraded performance as the number of users rises, it may be desirable to have data available locally so the end user can work faster.

To estimate storage requirements for a local area network, look at how much of a workstation's information access requirements involve shared data. If most of the data and applications will be provided by the file server, then a conventional disk drive or two may be sufficient. As the proportion of "local" work increases, the need for higher-capacity storage rises.

What Type of Work Will Be Performed at a Workstation?

Some types of work place heavy demands on mass storage. Word-processing operations, even within small organizations, can accumulate many megabytes of letters, proposals, and other documents in a short period of time. It is for that reason that so many word-processing operations are tied into a mini- or mainframe computer. Word processing is also a good candidate for networking.

However, stand-alone word-processing stations are gaining in popularity as microcomputers replace dedicated word processors at many organizations. But, how to account for the mass-storage needs of these workstations? A fixed disk drive has the capacity needed, but may limit flexibility. A given file can be revised only on the workstation on which that file resides. A fixed-disk-based work-processing setup would soon have too many operators vying for some workstations, while others went unused.

In such situations, the best solution might be to network all the workstations together. However, where that is not practical, it is still possible to gain many of the benefits of hard disks by storing the word-processing software on an internal fixed disk and using high-capacity diskettes or removable media (Bernoulli cartridges hold 10 MB and up) for the actual data files. You may also choose to select a given PC as the "home" workstation for a given group of files, and then take the time to copy the files to diskette for transfer to another PC when they must be worked on elsewhere.

A logbook or some other system to mark files that have been "checked out" should be used to insure that the "home" PC's file is updated when the work has been completed. As you can tell, such a solution is clumsy at best, which is why networking is almost the only reasonable solution for word-processing groups of more than two or three PCs.

Shared workstations aren't limited to word-processing departments. Even outside the clerical area you may find a limited number of PCs being used by many different people. Few companies have a PC for every manager who wants or can benefit from using one. Instead, they may have common workstations accessed by several different workers. Here, the ability to transport data files from machine to machine may be more important than capacity. But, again, higher capacities make such migration more convenient and efficient.

Summary

With such a wide array of options available today, anyone setting up an office automation system, or upgrading an existing configuration, should take into account all of the factors in choosing mass-storage options for microcomputers. You need to look at who will be using the workstation, what type of work will be done at the PC, and how the computer will be interfaced—or not—with other users.

Conventional disks, high-capacity disks, fixed disks, and their backup options (not discussed here, such as streaming tape), each have capabilities and limitations. By accurately estimating how much capacity you realistically need, and knowing how it will be used, you'll be in a better position to make the most cost-effective choice.

PART TWO
HARD DISK TIPS AND TRICKS

The following chapters go beyond the theoretical to provide you with practical information on how to set up, organize, and use your hard disk. You'll be able to preview—before you reach the point of no return—just what is involved in installing a hard disk on your own. We'll cover ways to configure your hard disk *now* to save you a great deal of time and trouble later on. There will be much useful information on DOS and how it can streamline your hard disk work, as well as a brace of useful utility programs that can simplify operations and speed up any repetitive fuctions.

7
Getting Started

In an ideal world, all hard disk drives would be purchased at a reasonable price either already installed in the computer or from a knowledgeable local dealer who would make the installation and lead the new user through all the intricacies of getting started using a hard disk. Often, this is not the case. We've run into overworked managers in large organizations who have purchased their own hard disks for a company computer just to gain the productivity tools. Self-employed individuals may be on a tight budget, and perceive buying a mail-order hard disk as a quick way to save $100 or so. Others may find their local dealer support lacking or live in a remote area beyond such aid.

For whatever reason, hard disk owners sometimes need a bit of guidance in getting their new storage device set up and working properly. They may also want to read through the various steps involved before deciding whether to do the job themselves or depend on a dealer's technicians.

This chapter will take you through the basics of installing and setting up your hard disk. Because there are so many different brands of disks and computers, the guidelines are necessarily general. However, since hard disk installation is not at all difficult, and the devices themselves usually come with instructions, most will find this chapter sufficient.

Installing Bay-Mount Hard Disks

Carefully remove the cover from your computer, watching for any cables, such as the floppy disk cables, that might catch on the cabinet as it slides off. If you don't own a battery-operated power screwdriver, now is a good time to invest $15 in one. Once you've experienced the productivity gains of a hard disk, you may find yourself removing the cover more often to install turbo boards, extended or enhanced memory, or other upgrades.

Next, determine what bay will be used to mount the hard disk. There may be a cover over an empty bay, which can be removed and saved. (You might want to sell the computer at some later date in its original configuration.) If you will be replacing a full- or half-height floppy disk, the floppy is usually held in place by two screws at one side or another. Remove them, and the drive will slide right out.

The floppy drive will have two cables attached. One will be a ribbon cable, which carries the data to and from the drive, and the other a wired connector carrying the power. Notice how they are oriented when you unplug them. Connectors are often "keyed" to keep the user from installing them incorrectly, but knowing in advance how they fit can eliminate fumbling later on.

If you are going from a two 360K floppy system to a single 360K floppy system, take out the A: and put the B: in its place. The two drives are not electrically identical, and substituting the B: for the A: will save you the bother of locating something called a terminating resistor in the B: and putting it in a socket on the A:. Should you elect to do this, your computer's guide to operations should tell you where the resistor is. In a pinch, you can compare the two drives; the resistor is colored differently—frequently white or blue—and one drive will have it and the other not, if they are of the same make.

Most half-height hard disk kits will come with a collection of brackets that will allow you to mount the drive in a full-height slot, along with bezels and faceplates to cover up the gap on the front of your computer. Slide the hard disk into place. Some hard disk instructions specify that a half-height drive be placed on the top or bottom, to allow proper operation. Follow the manufacturer's instructions.

Before sliding the hard disk in all the way, connect the data ribbon cable, which goes to the hard disk controller (not the same cable used for the floppy), and the power connector. If you are installing half-height floppies and a hard disk to keep both your floppy disk drives, you will need a "pigtail" Y-connector to allow power to go to all three devices. Such connectors are usually furnished with the hard disk.

Once the connections have been made, finish fastening the hard disk with the brackets supplied. Be certain that the disk is firmly installed, as you don't want it sliding around when the computer is moved.

If you have a computer with a built-in hard disk controller, route the data cable to the controller, and plug it in. If the cable connector is not keyed, the instructions that came with the hard disk will help you decide how to orient it.

Others will need to install the hard disk controller. If this controller will also handle the floppy disks, you will want to place it in the slot closest to the drive bays, for easy routing of the cable. Otherwise, it is often easier to place the shorter floppy disk controller in that slot, and the hard disk controller in the next one. Connect the data cable, and route it either around the back, under, or over the floppy disk controller card.

If you are installing more than one hard disk, your controller card can probably handle both. There will be an additional socket for the second data cable, and instructions with the controller will explain how to set up one disk as, say, C: and the second as D:.

There are a few more steps to follow. Some early hard disk kits included a ROM that had to be installed in a socket on the IBM PC. Very early PCs also needed a new ROM-BIOS to allow them to recognize hard disks at all. Install these if necessary. Chips on the system board are all oriented in the same direction: look for a mark or notch at one end of a chip you are installing, and see how the similar marks on the other chips in your computer are oriented.

If you have removed a floppy disk from your system, you may have to reset the system switches to let the computer know about the new configuration. These switches don't actually physically change any circuit paths on the PC; the computer simply looks to see how they are set and then makes its own adjustments as to how it operates accordingly. That's why later computers have been designed to replace the switch blocks with nonvolatile RAM configuration settings.

Those are the initial steps to installing a bay-mount hard disk.

Installing a Hard Disk Card

If you've read the previous section, you're about to learn why hard disk cards are so popular. Remove the cover as described before. Locate an empty slot or slots into which the hard disk card will fit. Carefully slide in the card, and tighten the mounting screw. Replace the cover on your computer.

Easy? Actually, we've oversimplified the installation. Some hard disk cards don't draw their power from the system board through the expansion slot. They require a power lead directly from the power supply, using a pigtail Y-connector. Also, if you have another hard disk already installed in your computer, you will need to check the instructions that come with the hard disk card. That card's controller may operate both. The instructions will specify which bay-mount hard disks are compatible. Follow them carefully in connecting the bay-mount disk's data cable to the hard disk controller card's extra connector. *Remove* the original hard disk controller.

You may also have to juggle cards around a bit to find a setup that will allow your hard disk card to use up the fewest number of slots. Some cards have overhang on both sides of the card, which can provide scant clearance in a PC-XT or other computer with narrower expansion slot spacing. You may want to move the computer's speaker to a new location and install the hard disk card in the end slot to give it room on both sides.

You might want to look for or make a special bracket that would allow you to mount a COM or LPT connector or two on the end plate facing the back of the computer. Many multifunction cards come with additional ports that are interfaced to the outside world through a bracket that can consume a needed slot. Since the hard disk card ordinarily doesn't have any outside connectors, you can gain double slot-duty by routing those ports through that slot's bracket.

External hard disk drives generally require only installing a card in the computer, and so will not be discussed separately.

Testing and Formatting

Don't put the cover back on your computer yet. A frequent error many make in installing a hard disk is to accidentally bump the system board switches (on computers that have them) when sliding in cards. Check and double-check their settings now. Then set the system unit to one side, connect the power, keyboard, and monitor, and turn the computer on.

The computer should run through its power-on self-test (POST), and you should hear a whirring sound as the hard disk comes up to speed. If the computer powers up, but the hard disk does not, check the power cable connections. If the computer powers up and then shuts down, it is likely that your hard disk and all the cards in your computer are putting too much current draw on the power supply. It is unlikely that this will show up at this stage, however. It is more probably that an anemic power supply will show up the first time you attempt to use one or two floppy disk drives at the same time the hard disk is running. (Just copy from A: to B: to test this.)

Don't put a diskette in drive A:. You want to see if the hard disk has been formatted and configured with DOS by the manufacturer. If so, the computer will run through the POST, then try to access drive A:. If no diskette is found there, and everything else is as it should be, the system will look for a hard disk and try to boot from that.

If you end up in cassette BASIC because DOS was unable to boot, you'll know that your hard disk has not been preformatted with DOS by the manufacturer. Boot the system from the same version of DOS that you will be installing on the hard disk. DOS 2.1 will work fine, but if you want to take advantage of the more efficient smaller cluster size, you should use DOS 3.0 or later.

There are two types of formatting that are done to hard disks. The first is the low-level format. This puts basic information on the disk, which allows DOS to format the disk and also allows the identifying and locking out of bad sectors. Every hard disk will have at least a few bad sectors. The manufacturer often performs the low-level format in certifying the disk, and may put a sticker on the disk identifying these bad sectors. Because low-level formatting is so often done for the end user, try the following steps first, using FDISK and FORMAT.

High-level formatting simply lays out the sectors and tracks, builds the FAT and root directory, and other structures needed to use the hard disk. Before this can be done, the hard disk has to be identified to DOS, using FDISK, a program supplied with the operating system. One of the things FDISK allows you to do is to set aside part of the hard disk for DOS, and part for another operating system, such as XENIX. While XENIX and UNIX-like systems should become more popular for personal computers as 80386 computers become more widespread, at present the vast majority of PCs are set up for DOS only. We'll deal only with the DOS aspects in this book. Users knowledgeable enough to cope with a more complex operating system like XENIX probably need less help in this area in any case.

Run FDISK, and view a list of options like the following:

```
Current Fixed Disk Drive: 1

Choose one of the following:
    1. Create DOS Partition
    2. Change Active Partition
    3. Delete DOS Partition
    4. Display Partition Date
    5. Select Next Fixed Disk Drive

Enter choice:_
```

DOS *partitions* are the logical areas of the drive set aside for a particular operating system. You might want to dedicate

60 percent for MS-DOS, and 40 percent for CP/M-86 or some other operating system. More likely, you will want to allocate the entire hard disk for MS-DOS.

Choose menu item 1 to create a DOS partition. You *might* see a message like, "DOS partition already created," in which case the hard disk has already been set up for you, even though DOS itself was not installed and you could not boot the drive. You might also find that FDISK refuses to recognize that you have a hard disk attached at all.

In this case, the low-level format was not done, or not done properly (the author has found this in nearly half of the hard disks he has installed). Get the utility disk that was furnished with the hard disk. There will be a program especially created to perform the the low-level format. Run it. You will probably be asked to enter the track and sector numbers of the bad sectors (printed on a label on the disk). Depending on the size of your hard disk and the formatting program, the low-level format can take ten minutes to several hours. That's why we tried to skip this step if it was already done. There is no danger in repeating the low-level format (unless you neglect to lock out bad sectors that have been locked out by the manufacturer), but it is time-consuming. Once the low-level format is complete, go back to FDISK and select menu item 1 again.

From there, you will see a menu like the following:

```
Create DOS Partition
Current Fixed Disk Drive: 1
Do you wish to use the entire fixed disk for DOS
(Y/N)?_
```

Most will reply "Y." FDISK will ask you to insert the DOS disk in A: and press a key. Next, you'll format the hard disk for MS-DOS by typing:

```
Format C: /S /V
```

The /S option tells DOS to install the operating system on the disk, while the /V option asks DOS to request a volume name after the disk has been formatted. Later versions of DOS have introduced ever more convoluted safeguards against accidentally formatting a hard disk, so you'll have to wend through requests to verify that you *do* want to format the disk, and, in later versions if a volume name has already been given, to verify the volume label.

Formatting will take a few minutes, again depending on the size of your hard disk. At the end, DOS will tell you that the system—consisting only of COMMAND.COM and the two invisible DOS files (IBMBIO.COM and IBMDOS.COM)—has been transferred. You'll be asked for a volume label.

Press Control-Alt-delete and see if your hard disk will now boot. If so, you are ready to begin organizing. If you have gotten as far as formatting, there is really little to have gone wrong, in any case.

For the techno-freaks, when the PC doesn't find a bootable disk in drive A:, it tries to find the first sector of the first surface on the first cylinder of the hard disk. This first sector contains a short bit of code called a partition loader, which tells the computer which partition is bootable. Each partition contains its own bootstrap loader as its first sector, so the PC goes to the first sector of the bootable partition, accesses the loader code, and proceeds to load the operating system.

FDISK allows you to divide the hard disk into one to four partitions, with only one active at any given time. Even if a partition is not bootable, you can still access it if you boot from the floppy disk or from the active partition and then use FDISK to change the active partition (menu item 2) before rebooting.

Other FDISK options that are even less frequently used allow you to select (and partition) a second hard disk, delete a DOS partition (you don't want to use XENIX anymore, say), or see your hard disk's partition data.

At this point, we've gotten your hard disk up and booting. Now its time to organize the disk in ways that will help you be the most productive. Even though you may just be getting started, there are things you can do *now* that will save a great deal of time and effort later on. The first step will be to learn something about DOS and the way it stores files and directories.

8
DOS

Any discussion of how to use a hard disk must start with the disk operating system—DOS. There are many different operating systems within the PC world, including UNIX and its XENIX variations, as well as Concurrent DOS and OS/2. With the introduction of 80386 computers, there have come a large group of operating systems tailored specifically to the capabilities of the 80386 system, sometimes in the guise of windowing environments, like *Desqview*.

However, the most commonly used operating systems for PCs are MS-DOS and PC-DOS. They are almost identical: PC-DOS is the version sold by IBM with its PCs, while MS-DOS is a more generic version provided with compatible computers. Many systems can run both, to a great extent.

There are some differences, chiefly because of the difference in the copyrighted ROMs supplied with IBM PCs. The IBM computers, for example, have part of BASIC incorporated in ROM, so the BASICA program provided with PC-DOS is actually a hybrid that mixes its own code with the ROM routines. Compatible computers must load BASIC entirely from a disk file, usually called GW-BASIC. IBM has also made some other minor changes to DOS to suit its own computers' need.

In general, a new release of MS-DOS and PC-DOS has come in response to each introduction of a new IBM product. Scan this list of the first seven DOS versions:

Release	Date	Product
1.0	8/81	IBM PC
1.1	5/82	Double-sided disk drives
2.0	3/83	IBM PC-XT
2.1	10/83	PCjr, half-height drives
3.0	08/84	PC-AT, 1.2 megabyte floppy
3.1	03/85	IBM PC Network
3.2	12/85	PC Convertible, 3.5-inch disks
3.3	4/87	1.44 megabyte 3.5 inch drives, PS/2

Each new version of DOS generally adds capabilities for new hardware, usually new types of disk drives. In addition, most later releases of DOS brought useful new features not dependent on hardware innovations. For example, DOS 2.0 improved on DOS 1.1 by providing the ability to install customized device drivers for more flexible interfacing of peripherals of all types. Extended keyboard and screen control allowed redefining keys and handling the screen more flexibly. DOS 3.0 brought the capability of marking files as read-only with the new ATTRIB command, and expanded the ways in which keyboard layout and date and time formats could be configured.

DOS 2.1 remained as a standard even after the introduction of DOS 3.0, because floppy disk users had little incentive to upgrade to an operating system that took up more memory and disk space, and offered few new features they could use, other than the ability to specify a label for a disk even after formatting had been completed. Hard disk users find more advantages in DOS 3.x, particularly with DOS 3.2 and later versions, which have interesting new features, such as DRIVER.SYS (which allows the user to create an alternate identifier for a drive).

Some of the techniques described in this book will require DOS 3.x or later, although the vast majority will work equally well with DOS 2.x. Where a special feature is unique to DOS 3.0, 3.1, 3.2, etc., that will be explained. We'll also assume that you already know basic DOS commands that are used with a floppy-disk-based sytem, such as FORMAT, COPY, DIR. We won't bore you with discussions on how to name files, use wildcards, or copy a file from one disk drive to another. However, other features of DOS are a bit obscure. For example, it is quite possible to use a floppy disk computer and never have encountered the concept of *subdirectories.*

If we treated the hard disk as an enormous floppy disk, only with 70 or so times the capacity, one problem would crop up immediately: we would soon have hundreds of files listed in a mammoth directory each time we typed DIR C:. You might give each type of file a particular extension, such as .TXT, .WKS, .LTR, .MEM, and so forth, and summon only groups of files by typing DIR C:*.TXT or some variation. For those with many small files, even this system still might result in a listing of hundreds of files. The system could become terribly cumbersome if carried to extremes. Certainly, creating file names like BUSCH01.LTR, BUSCH12.LTR, and so forth would allow you to retrieve lists of files using wildcards: DIR BUSCH*.LTR or DIR BUSCH1?.LTR would work just fine. However, simply keeping track of how the files would have to be named would be difficult and time-consuming. What hard disk users need is an arrangement like that automatically provided to floppy disk users: separate logical disks that can be used to group related files.

DOS versions after 2.0 provided for this with what is called a *hierarchical directory structure.* Imagine that your hard disk is a file cabinet. Any given drawer in the file cabinet is a DOS partition: you can only work with the contents of one active drawer, or partition, at a given time.

You might have a label on the outside of a drawer, providing a clue as to what the contents of that drawer might be. To simplify things, let's assume that the entire drawer (and the computer) is dedicated to one task, tracking personnel records for the entire corporation (it's a *very* large drawer).

The label on the outside of the drawer corresponds to the main, or *root,* directory of your hard disk. That label might be PERSONNEL, and then underneath that, would be a listing of the various folders within the drawer, broken down by some convenient classification, such as geographic area. So the major folder headings might be EAST, WEST, MIDWEST, and SOUTH. These headings would correspond to the major subdirectories listed in your root directory.

On the front of each folder might be further classifications. On the Midwest folder, there might be a label listing CHICAGO, KANSAS CITY, OMAHA, etc. Inside the Chicago folder, you might find individual envelopes with employee names. Because all the classifications are nested one inside each other in an arrangement that can be charted to look something like a tree, hierarchical directories are said to be *tree-structured*. Translated from a file cabinet to a computer, our directory structure might look something like this:

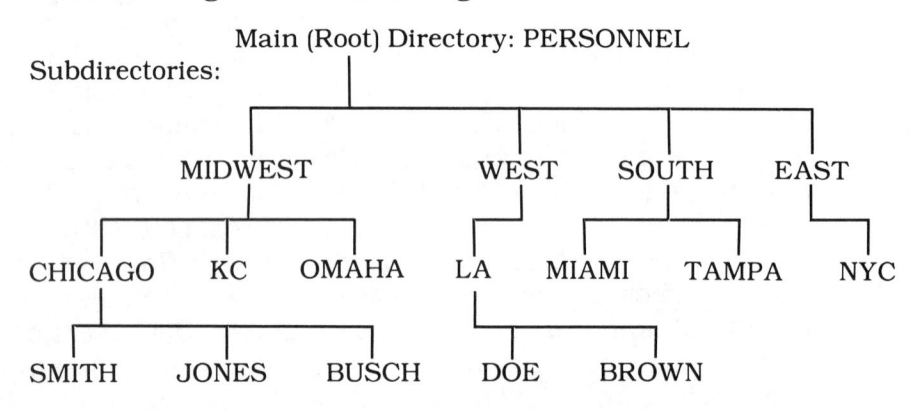

```
                    Main (Root) Directory: PERSONNEL
Subdirectories:                   |
        ┌─────────────┬───────────┴───┬──────────┐
     MIDWEST         WEST           SOUTH       EAST
        │             │               │           │
   ┌────┼────┐        │         ┌─────┴────┐      │
CHICAGO  KC  OMAHA    LA      MIAMI     TAMPA    NYC
   │                           │
┌──┴──┬─────┐              ┌───┴───┐
SMITH JONES BUSCH          DOE   BROWN
```

Nested within each directory may be one or more subdirectories containing files or other subdirectories. For example, in addition to the subdirectories like CHICAGO, KC, or OMAHA, the MIDWEST subdirectory may contain files of its own that pertain to the entire region: performance reports, sales for that region, and other information. The Chicago directory could contain summaries of data about that city's office.

When you are logged onto the root directory, the contents of the directories below are invisible to you. DIR will reveal only the names of the files in the root directory, plus the names of the subdirectories themselves. The latter always appear with the indication ⟨DIR⟩ in the size column, to indicate a subdirectory:

```
Volume in drive C: is PERSONNEL
Directory of C:
COMMAND.COM         22042      9-14-88   8:00a
WEST               <DIR>      10-15-88   9:02a
SOUTH              <DIR>      10-15-88   9:03a
MIDWEST            <DIR>      10-15-88   9:04a
EAST               <DIR>      10-15-88   9:04a
```

You are looking only at the root directory and its files, representing a tree that looks something like this:

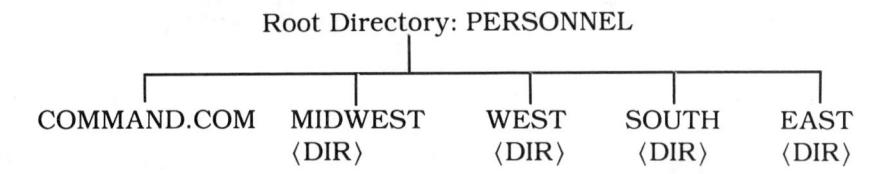

```
                   Root Directory: PERSONNEL
         ┌──────────────┬──────────┬──────────┬─────────┐
   COMMAND.COM      MIDWEST      WEST       SOUTH      EAST
                     <DIR>       <DIR>      <DIR>      <DIR>
```

DOS sees subdirectories as just special types of files. For example, when you type DIR *filename,* DOS shows you whether or not that file exists in the specified directory. The command

```
DIR C:\COMMAND.COM
```

would produce a display like this:

```
Volume in drive C: is PERSONNEL
Directory of C:
COMMAND.COM       22042     9-14-88   8:00a
```

However, when you type DIR *directoryname,* DOS will display the file names of the files *within* that subdirectory. For example, DIR MIDWEST would generate a screen display like this:

```
Volume in drive C: is PERSONNEL
Directory of C:\MIDWEST
    .            <DIR>      10-15-88   9:02a
    ..           <DIR>       9-14-88   8:00a
CHICAGO          <DIR>      10-15-88   9:08a
KC               <DIR>      10-15-88   9:08a
OMAHA            <DIR>      10-15-88   9:09a
```

However, to view the contents of a subdirectory, you must include the names of all the *parent* directories above it to provide DOS with the proper *path* to that directory. The subdirectory names are separated with a backslash, and the root directory is referred to simply with a backslash:

```
C>DIR \WEST
```

This would provide a listing of the contents (files or subdirectory names) of subdirectory WEST, which is one level down from the root directory, \. If you happened to be logged onto another drive, you would have to add the C:.

```
A>DIR C:\WEST
```

You can access directories several levels below by typing out the proper path to those files. To see all the files pertaining to SMITH, who works in Chicago, you would type:

```
C>DIR C:\MIDWEST\CHICAGO\SMITH\*.*
```

Moving through Directories

We can change the active directory from the root directory to one of the subdirectories with the CHDIR command. Most people just use the allowed abbreviation, CD. Go back to the root directory PERSONNEL (what you think of as the directory name of the root is actually the *volume* name or label applied by DOS after formatting, or by using the LABEL command). If you were to type CD SOUTH, and then DIR, you would see the following:

```
Volume in drive C: is PERSONNEL
Directory C:\SOUTH
    .           <DIR>        10-15-88   9:02a
    ..          <DIR>         9-14-88   8:00a
    MIAMI       <DIR>        10-15-88   9:11a
    TAMPA       <DIR>        10-15-88   9:12a
```

Note that subdirectory names have the same restrictions as file names: eight characters plus an optional three-character extension. Most users don't apply the extension, but otherwise you may have to abbreviate to fit the name you wish into the eight-character limitation. Subdirectories are actually stored by DOS as files, which is why the restrictions apply. The single dot entry represents the current directory. DIR . is the same as simply typing DIR alone. The double dot represents the next directory level up, or the parent directory.

Within a given directory, you may see the files in the directory above by typing *DIR ..* at the DOS prompt.

It is possible to jump from one subdirectory to another in great leaps by typing CD command and the correct path name. If you happened to be in subdirectory C:\MIDWEST\CHICAGO\SMITH and wanted to go back up the tree and down again to check on BROWN over in LA, you could type:

    CD\WEST\LA\BROWN

to get there in one jump.

Creating a Subdirectory

Subdirectories are created with the MKDIR, or MD, command. You may type MD *directoryname* to create a directory below the parent directory you are in. If the current directory was C:\MIDWEST\CHICAGO and new employee Green came on-board, you could just type:

    MD Green

From the root directory, it would have been simpler to type in:

    MD \MIDWEST\CHICAGO\GREEN

If a directory already exists by that name, or the name you have chosen is invalid, DOS will helpfully remind you.

Removing a Subdirectory

Directory names cannot be erased by normal DEL or ERASE commands. You must *first* erase all the files in that directory (ERASE CHICAGO, for example, will delete all the files, but *not* the subdirectories or *their* files in subdirectory CHICAGO), and then use the RMDIR, or RD, command:

    RD Chicago

DOS has a TREE command that will allow you to display the structure of all the directories in a hard disk system, and includes a /F option that will additionally show the files in those subdirectories.

However, at this point your hard disk has *no* subdirectories at all. This discussion was designed to explain the concept, allowing you to make a logical plan for your own particular directory structure. Examine your own needs closely to determine a logical, file-cabinet-type arrangement.

Many people find it convenient to store *only* the minimum files necessary to boot the hard disk in the root directory. These would include AUTOEXEC.BAT, COMMAND.COM, and CONFIG.SYS (all explained in more detail later). Then, the root directory's subdirectories would be created, based on the particular applications of the user. Here is a typical directory structure:

```
ROOT
    Subdirectories:
        BATCHES
        DOS
        LOTUS
            Subdirectories:
                WKS-ACCT
                WKS-TAX
                DRIVERS
                GRAPHICS
        COMM
        WP
            Subdirectories:
                LETTERS
                    86
                    87
                    88
                MEMOS
                REPORTS
                PROPOSALS
                STYLEFMT
        UTILITY
            Subdirectories:
```

                    SIDEKICK
                    OUTLINE
                    DOS

   Note that we don't really have two subdirectories named DOS. One is called C:\DOS, while the other is C:\UTILITY\DOS. Their full path names are different, and DOS would never get them confused, even if you might.

Naming Files

   To help make finding and manipulating files in subdirectories easier, it might be useful to review a few of the file-naming conventions. A file's true name includes its drive specifier (i.e., A:, B:, C:, etc.) as well as the *full* path name. That's why you can have two files on-line at one time with the same name if they are in different drives or directories. Both might be called TEST.DOC, but on closer examination, the full file names of each might be A:TEST,DOC, B:TEST.DOC, or B:\WP\TEST.DOC.
   The reason you don't always have to type the full file name is that DOS accepts certain values as *defaults* when they are not otherwise specified. For example, when you are logged onto A:, that drive specifier becomes the default. Should you type DIR JONES.DOC, DOS will assume you mean DIR A:JONES.DOC. Similarly, when logged onto a hard disk subdirectory, DOS will assign that directory's path name as the default.
   Thus, when logged onto C:\MIDWEST, you may type DIR JONES.DOC in order to see if C:\MIDWEST\JONES.DOC is there. If the desired file happened to called C:\MIDWEST\CHICAGO\SMITH.LTR and you were in subdirectory C:\MIDWEST, it would be necessary to type only DIR CHICAGO\SMITH.LTR; DOS would add the C:\MIDWEST automatically as the default.
   If no file specification is typed after a subdirectory name, DOS assumes that you are specifying *all* the files in that subdirectory. So you need type only DIR CHICAGO, and not DIR CHICAGO*.*, to view the contents of subdirectory CHICAGO.

Similarly, to ERASE the contents of an entire subdirectory, you may type ERASE CHICAGO instead of ERASE CHICAGO\ *.*. DOS will even ask you "Are you sure (Y/N)" exactly as if you had typed ERASE *.*.

Further, to COPY from one subdirectory to another or to another disk, you may specify a subdirectory name:

```
COPY CHICAGO B:
COPY CHICAGO ..
COPY CHICAGO ARCHIVE
COPY CHICAGO C:\MISC\FILES
```

The first example would copy all the files in subdirectory CHICAGO to B:, while the second would copy all the files in that subdirectory to the next highest, or parent, directory. The third example would copy the files to another subdirectory called ARCHIVE at the same level (that is, within the same parent directory). The last example would copy all the files to a subdirectory called C:\MISC\FILES.

Setting Up Paths

Starting with version 2.0 of MS-DOS and PC-DOS, the operating system automatically began searching through the PATH specified in something called the system *environment* when looking for files ending in the .COM, .EXE, and .BAT extensions. The environment is a special area of memory, usually only 528 bytes or so, that is reserved for storing information that can be accessed by DOS, various programs, and even simple files that you write yourself. This area of memory is not at all complex to understand or use, since the information stored there is in the form of variables and definitions. From the DOS prompt, type SET to see the current environment variables that have been defined. You may see something along these lines:

```
COMSPEC=C:\COMMAND.COM
PROMPT=$n$g
```

Don't be alarmed. These were set for you automatically by DOS when you booted up. However, simply by typing SET and a variable name and value, you may redefine the environment variable. Try typing SET PROMPT Hello There! Your system prompt will change from C⟩ (or A⟩, etc.) to *Hello There!* Now type SET alone on a line once more to see how the environment variable has been changed. To return your prompt to normal, just type PROMPT on a line by itself. Then type SET to see that the environment variable has been returned to its default. Certain of these variables have predefined uses, but you are not limited to using those variables alone. Type SET MYNAME.=PeeWee, then type SET to find your new contribution to DOS's environment. There are ways for programs and files that you create to access the variables to check for certain conditions.

There is one important environment variable that is useful to hard disk users—PATH. This variable provides a listing of the disk drives and subdirectories that should be searched for system files (the .COM, .EXE, and .BAT files previously mentioned) if the file is not found in the current directory. You may string them together in the order to be searched, separated by semicolons. From the command line, type:

```
SET PATH=C:\;A:\
```

Actually, in the case of the variables with predefined functions, typing SET is optional. DOS doesn't allow using PATH, PROMPT, or COMSPEC variables for any other purpose, so you may type them alone without using SET. The command

```
PATH=C:\;A:\
```

would produce exactly the same results: causing DOS to search, first the current directory for a system file, and then C:\ and A:\. (Type SET to see your new environment variable.) This is a powerful capability, because it allows us to store frequently used files in subdirectories of our choosing on the hard disk, and still allows DOS to find them no matter *what* subdirectory we happen to be using at the moment. For that reason, many users like to copy all their DOS files (the external commands like FORMAT.COM and utilities) to a subdirectory called DOS. By keeping them separate, it is easy to update a

91

hard disk to a new version of DOS, simply by using the SYS command and then copying all the other programs over to the DOS subdirectory.

You may also elect to keep batch files separate in a BATCHES subdirectory, and other programs in their own directories. A simple PATH command will tell DOS exactly where to look:

    PATH=C:\;C:\DOS;C:\BATCHES

If you keep no files in the root directory, the first specification can be left off entirely, It is not a good idea to have a PATH command that includes too many subdirectories. If a file does not reside in any of the listed directories, either because it does not exist at all or you made a typo when you entered the name, or it resides in some other directory, DOS can waste a lot of time hunting through a long list of subdirectories specified by PATH. It's better to keep those specified to a few. Most people put the PATH command in their AUTOEXEC.BAT file so the environment is set properly as soon as they boot the computer.

In the next chapter we'll explore ways of tailoring your system through tools like the AUTOEXEC.BAT file, and present a sample file you can use as a model in configuring your own system.

9
Tailoring Your Hard Disk

The last chapter provided some vital background, necessary after formatting your hard disk. You now know most of what you need to structure and set up your hard disk properly. The next steps are for you to:

1. Decide on a basic subdirectory structure. This need not be cast in stone. You can always set up a new system of directories and copy files over to them later. But some planning now can save you that trouble in the future.
2. COPY the DOS programs over to your DOS subdirectory. We'll assume that you have named that directory DOS; if you choose some other name, make the substitution in the later examples.
3. COPY any working programs and files over to the subdirectories where they will be used. Your word-processing program may reside in its own subdirectory, C:\WP, with a collection of subdirectories below used for different types of files: C:\WP\LETTERS, C:\WP\MEMOS, etc. Or you may structure the subdirectories by accounts, clients, departments, etc.
4. Create CONFIG.SYS and AUTOEXEC.BAT files that will set up your system the way you want it when DOS boots.

You should be able to carry out the first three steps on your own. Here are more detailed instructions for the last.

Creating a CONFIG.SYS File

CONFIG.SYS is nothing more than an ASCII text file that DOS checks when the system boots, in order to determine how to configure the system. DOS does this *before* it runs the AUTOEXEC.BAT program. Unlike AUTOEXEC.BAT, only certain commands can be included in CONFIG.SYS; you can't carry out functions, such as changing the system prompt or asking DOS to RUN a program, for example. Each new release of DOS since DOS 2.0 has incorporated new CONFIG.SYS options. Among the commands you can include are the following:

- BUFFERS=nn. This allows setting aside from 1 to 99 areas of memory, each 528 bytes long, for temporary storage of disk input and output. Every time DOS reads the disk, it will gather up the amount of information specified by BUFFERS. If the next information requested by DOS has already been read into the buffer, then the data can be pulled very rapidly from the buffer memory, rather than from disk through a comparatively slow disk access. We've already seen that disk I/O can be a major factor limiting the speed of any PC.

    Buffers are used to substitute faster RAM access for slower disk access. An appropriate number of buffers can speed up operation of your program by allowing DOS to "cache" in memory some of the data that will be needed. DOS also stores information that will be written to disk until the buffer is full, thereby minimizing disk writes. However, too many buffers can slow down operation as much as too few. If your program needs to read a large number of short, scattered records, DOS will find itself wasting time reading a large block of information from disk when it needs only very little, but searching through the entire buffer for data can, in some cases, take longer than simply reading the information from the disk.

Without a BUFFERS=nn command in your CONFIG.SYS file, DOS defaults to two or three buffers, depending on your computer. Most hard disk users can benefit from 16 to 20 buffers; those with very fast hard disks may want to try 30 buffers or more. The key is to experiment to see what works best for you.

- FILES=nn specifies the number of files DOS may have open for use at any one time. You may use this configuration command to specify that number (and, in later versions of DOS, use FCBS to determine the number of file control blocks). DOS assumes eight files and four FCBS as the default. These are enough for most applications, but some may specify in their installation instructions the need for more. Follow those guidelines.
- BREAK=ON (or BREAK=OFF) lets you control how fast DOS responds when you press the Control-C or Control-Break key combination. Normally, DOS checks for these keys only when accessing a disk. If BREAK=ON, however, DOS will stop the current program immediately. Without BREAK switched on, you may find it rather difficult to interrupt programs that don't access the disk frequently. Some programs switch off BREAK on purpose, as it can be done from the DOS command line as well as with CONFIG.SYS. You may use either method to set BREAK the way you want it.
- DEVICE=*driver* is a command that allows you to tell DOS where to find a specific device driver for access to devices not built *into* DOS itself. These devices may be printers, video displays, mass-storage devices, or other peripherals.

For example, the keyboard is a device that is normally controlled by DOS using its own built-in routine. If you want, you can use a different routine to control the codes DOS receives when keys are pressed on the keyboard. For example, your device driver could intercept the normal key codes and substitute a different set corresponding to the Dvorak key layout.

In fact, MS-DOS happens to be supplied with an alternate keyboard driver routine, called ANSI.SYS. When this driver is loaded, certain key combinations are intercepted and new codes set to DOS. We can use these combinations to do a number of tricks with DOS, which will be covered in a later chapter. For right now, simply be aware that including a line in your CONFIG.SYS file like:

```
DEVICE=ANSI.SYS
```

will tell DOS to use that device driver after booting up.

There are many other useful drivers available. Versions of DOS after 3.0 are supplied with a driver called VDISK.SYS, which allows you to set up a RAM disk. VDISK also works with DOS 2.x, but you must either key in the assembler code yourself or purchase DOS 3.0 or later to legally acquire this driver. Note that only CONFIG.SYS has to reside in the root directory of your hard disk. The device drivers may be tucked away in a subdirectory, and specified:

```
DEVICE=C:\DOS\ANSI.SYS
DEVICE=C:\DOS\VDISK.SYS 100
```

More than one device driver can be listed in a CONFIG.SYS file. Some device drivers, such as VDISK.SYS, allow you to specify them more than once, thus setting up two or more different RAM disks.
- SHELL=*command processor*, /P, /E:⟨size⟩ allows you to specify the size of the DOS environment, which was discussed briefly in the last chapter. If you use many environment variables, the available space to store those variables may be used up. The command processor will usually be COMMAND.COM, and ⟨size⟩ should be replaced with the number of 16-byte increments to be set aside, if you are using DOS 3.1. DOS 3.1 defaults to a value of 10 (160 bytes), and you can specify no more than 62, for a total of 992 bytes. DOS 3.2 requires specifying ⟨size⟩ in bytes, and allows entries up to 32,767 bytes. The /P option makes the specification entered by SHELL permanent.

TAILORING YOUR HARD DISK

- COUNTRY=xxx makes it possible to specify the keyboard layout of your computer, if you wish to use an arrangement other than the default USA arrangement. Since CONFIG.SYS is an ASCII text file, you may create it with any word processor having an ASCII or nondocument mode. Or, since the file is generally short, you can type it in from the keyboard. Type:

```
COPY CON:CONFIG.SYS <Enter>
DEVICE=C:\DOS\ANSI.SYS
...
...
etc.
(Press F6 and <Enter> when finished.)
```

You can't edit CONFIG.SYS if it is typed from the console in this manner. To make changes, simply type COPY CON:CONFIG.SYS ⟨Enter⟩ again and retype the file with the alterations you want.

Creating AUTOEXEC.BAT

AUTOEXEC.BAT is another ASCII file, run by DOS immediately after CONFIG.SYS is read. This is a standard batch file and can contain any of the commands found in other batch files.

What's a batch file? It is a special kind of text file, which always contains the extension .BAT. That extension makes batch files a type of system file like those ending with .EXE or .COM. System files can be summoned simply by typing their *root* name—the part of the name before the extension. For example, you may run BASIC.COM or FORMAT.COM just by typing BASIC or FORMAT.

When DOS sees a file name consisting of a legal name with no extension, it first looks to see if a .COM or .EXE file (in that order) with that root exists. If so, it runs that program. Next, it looks to see if a .BAT file has that root. In that case, DOS then interprets each line of text in the batch file and tries to carry it out as if it were entered at the keyboard. If no .COM or .EXE or .BAT file with the root exists, and there is no other file by that name (if there is an extension, such as .BAS, it will not match), then the "Bad command or file name" error message is displayed.

So you can see that a batch file, called D.BAT, consisting of a single line, DIR A:, would cause DOS to display a directory of drive A: each time you typed in D⟨Enter⟩ at the keyboard—that is, as long as you did not have a file called D.EXE or D.COM in that disk directory. Since DOS always looks for the .COM and .EXE extensions first, you could not use batch files called FORMAT.BAT or BASIC.BAT in the same directory as FORMAT.COM or BASIC.COM (although you could *rename* the .COM files to something else). Batch files using the same root name as a DOS internal command are not allowed. You could not use a COPY.BAT or DIR.BAT, because those root names are reserved, among system file names, for DOS internal commands. Note that batch files with these names can be created. However, DOS will not *run* them.

There are a series of special batch commands that can be used, making up a special batch file command language; it will be covered in more detail later in this book.

AUTOEXEC.BAT follows the same rules as other batch files, except that DOS has been told to look for it automatically when starting up. If present in the root directory of your hard disk, DOS will carry out the commands in AUTOEXEC.BAT automatically without your needing to do anything.

AUTOEXEC.BAT is a good way to custom-configure your system the way you want it. You can choose the program that you want the computer to run when it is turned on. For example, if you want the PC to operate as an unattended host computer during certain hours of the night, you may connect it to a timer and auto-answer modem, and insert the name of your host communications program in the AUTOEXEC.BAT file. Then, when the timer turns the computer on, the host program will be run automatically.

AUTOEXEC.BAT can also be used to run utilities that set the system clock to a clock board you've installed, activate a RAM drive (if different from DOS 3.0's VDISK), or do other tasks on power-up. Each person's AUTOEXEC.BAT file will be different. You will want to start with a small one now, and perhaps add to it as you gain hard disk proficiency. Here's an example of a typical file, with a line-by-line description of what it does. You can use this as a model to add features to your own system (substituting your own clock program name, for example), as required. Later chapters will show how to do some of the trickier techniques, such as redefining keys:

```
SAMPLE AUTOEXEC.BAT
1.    echo off
2.    c:\dos\astclock
3.    path c:\batches;c:\dos;c:\
4.    C:\dos\nokey
5.    CD \
6.    CD DOS
7.    SK
8.    CD \
9.    echo AT S0=0 >COM1:
10.   ECHO ON
11.   PROMPT=$e[0;30;"DIR A:";13p
12.   PROMPT=$e[0;46;"DIR C:";13p
13.   PROMPT=$e[0;25;"C:\BATCHES\COM";13p
14.   PROMPT=$e[0;17;"C:\BATCHES\W";13p
15.   PROMPT=$e[0;50;"C:\BATCHES\MCI";13p
16.   PROMPT=$e[s$e[2;53H$p$e[1;53H$t$h$h$h$h$h$h
      $d$e[u$n$g
17.   ECHO OFF
18.   NOPARITY
19.   CLS
20.   cd\batches
21.   erase b:mci.asc
22.   erase c:\wp\mci.txt
23.   COMM S2
24.   CD\
25.   W
```

Please note that line numbering is for reference only.

Line 1: Turns off screen display.

Line 2: Activates the clock program used with the AST SixPakPlus multifunction board. Users of computers such as the PC-AT with a built-in system clock accessible to DOS won't need this line. Those with other multifunction boards will need to substitute the name of their own clock-reading program.

Line 3: Sets the PATH in the system environment that informs DOS how to look for batch files, .COM, and .EXE programs on the hard disk.

Line 4: First of several lines that activate various utility programs. NOKEY is a program that allows you to run Lotus *1-2-3* and other copy-protected programs from a hard disk, without the need to have a key disk in A:, and without the bother of special "installation" programs. This program remains in memory during an entire session, and so is loaded at start-up, rather than when loading Lotus, because certain other memory-resident programs like to be loaded in memory last. This procedure helps avoid potential problems.

Lines 5 and 6: Show an excessively roundabout way of changing the current working directory to C:\DOS; CD C:\DOS would have done the same thing).

Line 7: It was necessary to change the directory because *Sidekick*, loaded here, likes to be installed from the current directory.

Line 8: Changes the directory back to the root, once *Sidekick* is resident in memory.

Line 9: Serves a dual purpose. It directs a modem command to a Hayes-compatible modem, telling it to *not* answer the phone. If the modem is switched off, DOS prompts with the "Abort, Retry, Ignore" message that signals that the modem has not been switched on. The user can then flip the modem power switch and press "R" for Retry. If the modem is already on, it is commanded *not* to answer the phone so that the user can receive incoming calls on that line, but still use the active modem to dial out with *Sidekick's* dialer feature. *Note:* You can also put a Hayes command in your telecommunications software start-up batch file that turns auto-answer back on should you wish to receive a call. The same batch file can turn auto-answer back off when you exit telecommunications.

Line 10: Turns ECHO back on, since the following PROMPT commands (explained in the next chapter) only work when the output is displayed on the screen.

Line 11: Redefines Alt-A to send DIR A: to DOS when pressed.

Line 12: Redefines Alt-C to send DIR C: to DOS when pressed.

Line 13: Redefines Alt-P to provide a string that calls up COM.BAT, a batch file that loads a communications program.

Line 14: Alt-W is defined to call up a word-processing program (through W.BAT).

Line 15: Alt-M is defined to load a special batch file that loads the telecommunications program and triggers a special script that dials MCI mail, logs on, and downloads waiting mail.

Line 16: Redefines the system prompt so that the date and time and current directory appear in the upper right-hand corner of the screen.

Line 17: Turns ECHO back off.

Line 18: Clears the screen again.

Line 19: Invokes a utility program that shuts off parity checking, or random memory errors. With parity checking switched on, it is remotely possible that your computer could lock up because of a memory error. If you are running number-intensive programs, like Lotus *1-2-3*, you would probably want to be alerted should such an error occur. If the corrupted memory was in your spreadsheet in some unknown location, the entire spreadsheet could be inaccurate. A lock-up, while drastic, is better than losing $10,000 somewhere in your spreadsheet because of a memory error that has gone unnoticed.

Writers, on the other hand, don't care much if a character or two is mislaid. A good spelling checker will find the problem. What we don't want is for the computer to lock up after we've typed for an hour or two and forgotten to SAVE our work. So, such folk may want to automatically turn parity checking off with a public-domain program like NOPARITY.

Line 20: Since an AUTOEXEC.BAT file is always run when the user first turns the computer on, it can be used to perform a regular once-a-day task. Here, the current directory is changed to C:\BATCHES.

Line 21: Erases B:MCI.ASC, if it exists.

Line 22: Erases C:\WP\MCI.TXT, if it exists. (In lines 21 and 22, a "File not found" message is harmlessly displayed otherwise.) Killing these files is necessary because the particular telecommunications software and word-processing software won't function in the intended manner if the files are already present when they try to create them.

Line 23: Loads the telecommunications software

(PC-TALK III) with the S2 parameter that tells PC-TALK III to immediately begin carrying out the function stored in Shift-F2. That procedure is a function of PC-TALK III, rather than DOS.

Your own telecommunications software probably has a similar function key and "script" capabilities. In this case, the S2 function key dials up MCI mail, logs on, opens a disk file called MCI.ASC, reads the user's MCI INBOX, and logs off. At this point, a file has been created on B: called MCI.ASC with the contents of the messages. The user must then manually exit PC-TALK III, at which point the batch file picks up again.

Line 24: Calls W.BAT, loading word-processing software (or substitute your own "standard" application). The user is ready to begin the working day.

Most often, the next step would be to press a macro key within the word-processing software that creates a document called MCI.TXT and loads the ASCII file MCI.ASC into that, paginates it, and presents it to be read.

If a user reboots during the day for some reason, the last portion of the AUTOEXEC.BAT file can be avoided simply by turning the modem power switch off. Or a PAUSE command could be inserted after line 19 to provide the opportunity to press Control-C and abort the batch file at that point.

This sample AUTOEXEC.BAT file was provided to spark some ideas for building your own version tailored for your particular needs. Here are some other ideas:

1. Create a RAM disk using VDISK.SYS and CONFIG.SYS, or some other RAM disk program. Insert a line or two in the AUTOEXEC.BAT file to COPY some frequently used programs over to the RAM disk:

```
COPY C:\UTIL\*.* D:>NUL
COPY C:\BATCHES\*.BAT D:>NUL
```

The >NUL at the end redirects the printing of DOS messages to the screen during the copy process: a convenience. If you then include D:\ as your first directory in the PATH command, DOS will always search that memory disk first before checking the others specified. Depending on your application, you may find that the RAM disk access is even faster for frequently used utilities than the hard disk.

2. Embed these two lines as the last in your AUTOEXEC.BAT file:

```
PAUSE
CTTY COM1
```

When *you* boot up and receive the PAUSE message, press Control-C to send the batch file and continue with your work. If some unauthorized user were to boot your computer from the hard disk, they would probably just press a key when asked by the PAUSE command—in which case the computer would lock up (CTTY COM1 redirects control of the computer to one of your serial ports). They would have to reboot (pressing Control-C at the proper time) or boot from an ordinary DOS disk in drive A: to gain control of the computer.

Because this method is fairly easy to get around, it can be safely used only in an office environment of unsophisticated PC users. We'll present some more sophisticated security measures later on. However, for now, you've managed to get your hard disk computer up, configured, and running. Now let's use some of that power.

10
Getting DOS to Work for You

Many of the things we do with hard disks require carrying out a number of steps in a predictable order. For example, each time a particular word-processing program is run, it may be necessary to first log over to drive C: (if you happen to have been logged to another drive), change to the word-processing subdirectory, load a memory-resident dictionary or thesaurus program, and then type a command that activates the word-processing software. Of course, when you leave the program, you'll want to exit the WP subdirectory. Rather than type all these commands in each time such a series of operations is carried out, we can create a batch file to do them for us. A sample file, WP.BAT, might look like this:

```
ECHO OFF
C:
CD\WP
C:\UTIL\THESAURUS
WORDRITE C:\WP A:
CD\
```

Note that some word-processing programs, such as the fictitious one used in the preceding example, allow you to put one or more *parameters* on the command line, providing information that is passed along to the program. This may include the names of subdirectories where the word-processing program files are stored, and/or the name of the disk drive or subdirectory where text files are to be stored. Programs like *DisplayWrite 4* permit passing along the name of a configuration file to be used to set up a customized profile, as well as specifying alternate paths for program files and temporary files. Activating a program like this is almost impossible without an appropriate batch file.

With WP.BAT safely ensconced in our C:\BATCHES subdirectory, and an appropriate PATH command activated to point to that subdirectory, we can simply type WP when logged onto any drive or directory to start up the word-processing program. WP.BAT has become, for all intents and purposes, a new DOS command available for instant access. It is possible to incorporate other series of commands into batch files to tailor your own custom-designed DOS commands. For example, if you wanted to see, in turn, the directories of all the disks online in your system, you could create a batch file, called DIRS.BAT, with the following lines:

```
ECHO OFF
DIR A:
DIR B:
DIR C:
```

or

```
ECHO OFF
DIR A: \P
DIR B: \W
DIR C:\WP\*.TXT
DIR C:\WP\MEMO*.TXT
```

As you can see, the new command, summoned by typing DIRS, can be tailored quite precisely to your own particular needs. Batch files can be even more flexible because they can include not only the same commands that you type from DOS, but some additional, lesser-known commands that make up a rudimentary batch file language. These are in most cases not different from "regular" DOS commands, but they don't have many applications outside batch files. You may, for example, type:

```
ECHO Hello there!
```

GETTING DOS TO WORK FOR YOU

from the DOS command line, and the operating system will obediently display "Hello there!" on the screen. That's not particularly useful.

There are only a few batch file subcommands, but they can be used in many powerful ways, especially with one nonstandard extension that will be introduced later in this chapter. The key commands are:

- ECHO. Displays the message that follows on the screen. Unlike PRINT in BASIC, no quotation marks are needed. Example:

```
ECHO Please insert a new diskette in Drive A:
```

The ECHO subcommand may also be used in several additional ways. ECHO OFF will turn off the display of batch file commands as the commands are carried out. ECHO ON will turn on the display of the commands. When printed on a line by itself, ECHO will display the current ECHO status (either ON or OFF).

For example, compare these two batch files and their respective screen outputs.

```
File 1

ECHO OFF
Dir A:*.TXT
ECHO Insert Disk
PAUSE


File 2

DIR A:*.TXT
ECHO Insert Disk
PAUSE
```

Screen 1

```
ECHO OFF

Volume in drive A has no label
Directory of A:\
MEMOS    TXT    11264    2-24-87   11:34a
CAP      TXT    27648    2-24-87   10:36a
```

HARD DISK SOLUTIONS WITH BATCH FILE UTILITIES

```
        2       File(s)         146432 bytes free
Insert Disk
Strike a key when ready . . .
```

Screen 2

```
ECHO DIR A:*.TXT
 Volume in drive A has no label
 Directory of  A:\

MEMOS    TXT     11264   2-24-87  11:34a
CAP      TXT     27648   2-24-87  10:36a
        2 File(s)     146432 bytes free
ECHO Insert Disk
Insert Disk
PAUSE
Strike a key when ready . . .
```

The two examples differ only in the presence of ECHO OFF as the first line in the first batch file. ECHO OFF is first in most batch files, inserted to reduce the confusion and clutter on the screen while the batch file operates. The key exception is in the case of specialized files using the PROMPT command to pass certain keystrokes to the ANSI.SYS device driver. ECHO must be ON for ANSI.SYS to recognize the special codes (examples illustrating this will follow later).

In earlier releases of DOS, it was possible to print a blank line in a batch file by including ECHO, followed by two or more spaces. (ECHO alone returns the ECHO status, remember.) That nondocumented feature became a nonfeature with DOS 3.0 and later versions. A semiblank line can be incorporated by putting nothing but a period after the ECHO statement. A completely blank line can be inserted by telling DOS to print an invisible character such as ASCII 255. To enter that character (or any nonkeyboard character), hold down the Alt key while typing the character's code on the numeric keypad (not the row of numbers at the top of the keyboard). Special characters of that sort will be indicated with the ⟨alt-255⟩, ⟨alt-7⟩ designation in the batch files used in this book.

- PAUSE. This command will cause the batch file to suspend execution until the user presses a key. The pause can be used to allow operators to change their mind, insert a disk, or do some other task. Examples:

```
ECHO Press Control-C to Abort Batch File Now
PAUSE

ECHO Insert Volume 2 Disk in Drive A:
PAUSE
```

- GOTO. Like GOTO in BASIC, this subcommand sends control of the batch file to a different line. However, since line numbers are not used, a *label* is used instead. Labels must start with a colon, and are used by DOS only to find the relevant portion of the batch file. Everything else on a label line is ignored. This batch file shows examples of GOTOs and labels:

```
ECHO OFF
GOTO DIRECTORY
ECHO This line is never called.
:DIRECTORY
DIR A:
GOTO END
ECHO This line is never called, either.
:END Anything else on this line is ignored.
CLS
```

- REM. Allows you to insert remarks in your batch files. Anything after REM on a line is ignored. Example:

```
REM This line will be ignored by DOS if ECHO is OFF.
REM If ECHO is ON, DOS will display the line.
 :  This is also a remark, masquerading as a label.
 :  DOS will not display this remark even if ECHO is ON.
```

As you can see, labels can also double as remarks and, in fact, generally provide a less cluttered appearance in the batch file. As a bonus, labels don't ECHO to the screen even when ECHO is ON. In this book, we will use labels instead of REMs for those reasons.

- IF. This is a "crippled" version of IF as used in BASIC and other languages. IF may test *only* for three conditions:

1. Whether one string equals another.
2. Whether a file by a given name exists.
3. What the current ERRORLEVEL is.

In the first case, the strings must match to be considered identical. You may follow IF with NOT to test for "not equal," but the ⟨, ⟩, and ⟨⟩ string comparisons of BASIC are not allowed in batch files.

In addition, a double equals sign must be used. This convention is borrowed from languages which, unlike BASIC, make the proper distinction between equals used to *assign* values, and equals used to express *equivalence*. Consider the following examples:

```
A=B
IF A==B GOTO END
```

In the first case, A will *always* equal B after the line is run, because the value of A is assigned to B by that line. In the second case, no such assignment takes place. Instead, the line merely checks to see if the two are equal and, if so, performs some other task. Variables cannot be assigned in batch files, so only the double equals sign is used (unless you want the equals character to be displayed on the screen for some reason). Examples:

```
IF "Hello There"=="Hello There" GOTO END
IF NOT "Hello There"=="Hi" GOTO END
IF Notice No Quotes==Notice No Quotes GOTO END
```

Quotation marks are not required for string comparisons in batch files, but there is a reason for using them that will be explained shortly.

IF can check to see if a file already exists within a given directory or disk. This is useful in order to keep from overwriting files used by batch routines. You can also use this as a sort of "flag," by creating and erasing dummy files with certain names depending on a status you want to convey to the batch file. Examples:

```
IF EXIST A:DATABASE.DOC GOTO DONOTERASE
IF EXIST A:FLAG.$$$ GOTO END
```

ERRORLEVEL is a code set by DOS when certain errors occur during the execution of a command. IF can also check for the ERRORLEVEL status within a batch file. However, only a limited number of DOS commands actually set the ERRORLEVEL, so this test has limited utility by itself. However, there is an enhancement—a tiny machine-language program called INPUT.COM that does nothing more than wait for the user to press a key, and then set the ERRORLEVEL to the *scan code* of that key.

Scan codes are different from ASCII codes in many cases, because these codes can also indicate whether a second key, such as Shift, Control, or Alt, was pressed at the same time. So the letter A (ASCII 65) is represented by a scan code of 97 when pressed alone (this is the lowercase *a*), 65 when pressed with the Shift key, and 1 if pressed along with the Control key. Each key on the keyboard has its own code. In the case of the special keys, such as the function keys, cursor control keys, and *any* of the keys when pressed in combination with the Alt key, the scan code has *two* parts: a zero, followed by the code.

Thus, F1 has a scan code of 0,59 when pressed alone; 0,84 when pressed with the Shift key; 0,94 when pressed with the Control key; and 0,104 when pressed with the Alt key. A list of scan codes is provided in Appendix A of this book.

INPUT.COM will allow the user to enter any of the alpha keys A–Z, or the number keys 0–9. It will set the ERRORLEVEL to the scan code of the *shifted* alpha keys. Lowercase and uppercase A will both return an ERRORLEVEL of 65. Zeros in the scan code are ignored. So, F7 will also return an ERRORLEVEL of 65. Be on the lookout for these duplicates when writing your own batch files.

Note: There are many public-domain utilities equivalent to INPUT.COM. Some allow you to enter a prompt as part of the command, and may have other enhancements as well. In order to allow the utilities in this book to work with those programs, not only INPUT.COM, the batch files presented here all check for both uppercase and lowercase input. However, INPUT.COM automatically changes lowercase input to uppercase. The extra check is needed only to insure compatibility with these other INPUT.COM-like programs that do not perform this conversion.

INPUT.COM can be created by typing in the short BASIC program that follows:

```
10 OPEN "C:\INPUT.COM" AS #1 LEN = 1
20 FIELD #1,1 AS A$
30 FOR N=1 TO 20
40 READ B
50 LSET A$ = CHR$(B)
60 PUT #1
70 NEXT N
80 CLOSE
90 DATA 180,8,205,33,60,65,126,2,36,223,60
100 DATA 0,117,2,205,33,110,180,76,205,33
```

Store this in your DOS or BATCHES subdirectory. Use whichever subdirectory is checked *first*, after the current one, as specified by your PATH command. We'll use INPUT frequently in the utility batch files presented in this book.

The reason INPUT.COM is necessary is that there is no other easy way to make batch files *interactive*, that is, to allow user input after the file has begun to run. Batch command language has no equivalent of the BASIC INPUT statement and its variations, so you cannot have anything along these lines:

```
INPUT "ENTER YOUR NAME";variable
INPUT "ERASE ENTIRE HARD DISK (Y/N)?";variable
```

As you might guess, such a capability is invaluable. However, there are always tricks that can be used to get around the limitations of batch file language. For example, you may *redirect* the output of the PAUSE subcommand to a file in order to allow the user to enter choices from, say, a menu:

```
ECHO OFF
: [*] MENU.BAT [*]
ECHO  Enter Choice:
ECHO   1. Run Word Processing Program.
ECHO   2. Run Database Program.
ECHO   3. Run Spreadsheet.
PAUSE>NEXTPROG.BAT
NEXTPROG
```

The user will be presented with a menu of options, and asked to press a key corresponding to the selection. Then PAUSE will display the "Strike a key when ready...." prompt.

Any key the user then presses will be *redirected* into a batch file called NEXTPROG.BAT. That is, if they press the one key, then NEXTPROG.BAT will contain nothing but the number 1. If they press 2, the file will contain a 2, and so forth. The next line then *calls* the batch file, NEXTPROG.BAT, which in turn will attempt to call a batch file called 1.BAT, 2.BAT, etc. You can set up 1.BAT ahead of time to call up your word-processing program, 2.BAT to run the database, etc.

The chief drawback of this method is that it is impossible to set up an error trap to prevent the user from pressing some other key (4, or &, or whatever), which will then trigger an error when DOS is unable to locate &.BAT. You *could* set up separate batch files for every possible wrong key, which would themselves call back MENU.BAT, but this method is extremely clumsy.

Instead, INPUT.COM can allow you to enter a single keystroke, and the batch file can test for the ERRORLEVEL. The only complication is that IF ERRORLEVEL will not tell you whether the ERRORLEVEL is exactly a given value, but only whether it is that value or *higher.* So

```
IF ERRORLEVEL 51
```

would evaluate as true for *any* ERRORLEVEL 51 or higher. To test for a specific value, we have to nest a second test to see if the ERRORLEVEL is, in fact, higher than the one we are looking for. Example:

```
IF ERRORLEVEL 51 IF NOT ERRORLEVEL 52 GOTO THREE
ECHO You did NOT press 3!
GOTO END
:THREE
ECHO You pressed 3 (Scan Code 51)
ECHO Or, maybe, Shift Pg Dn (Scan Code 51)
:END
```

Because no ON...GOTO or similar constructs exist in batch file language, there is no simple way, even with INPUT.COM, to send control to various subroutines within the batch file after the file has started. A series of IF ERRORLEVEL statements, while lengthy, can do the job.

- FOR...IN...DO. This subcommand is the closest thing batch file language has to the FOR...NEXT loop of BASIC. A variable, designated by double percent signs, is sequentially assigned a value, and then the operation specified after DO is carried out. Operation will become clearer if you examine the following example:

```
FOR %%a IN (*.*) DO ERASE %%a
```

Each time through the loop, variable %%a will be assigned a different file name represented by *.*, whereupon that file will be erased. This particular example is a diabolical perversion of the ERASE *.* command, since in this case, DOS will *not* ask "Are you sure (Y/N)?"

You may separate items within the parentheses by spaces to include many different specifications for the set:

```
FOR %%a IN (C:\WP\*.DOC C:\ARC\MEM*.*) DO COPY A:
```

Using Environment Variables in Batch Files

It is also possible to substitute different kinds of variables and parameters for the items in the set. This is as good a time as any to reintroduce the environment variables discussed earlier.

You'll recall that SET could be used to define a variable in the special area of memory called the environment. PATH is one such variable and is used by DOS to determine which directory paths will be checked for system files. However, you may define variables of your own, for use by your programs and batch files. To incorporate such a variable in the batch file, we need only surround it by percent signs.

Assume that your batch file or some other program had defined an environment variable called DELFILES as equaling "C:\WP*.DOC." If you type SET all by itself, you might see (along with other variables) the following:

```
DELFILES=C:\WP\*.DOC
```

Your batch file could then include the following:

```
FOR %%a IN (%DELFILES%) DO ERASE %%a
```

What does this do for us? You do not have to explicitly state the specifier for the set that will be operated on by the FOR...IN...DO loop. Instead, you may just designate the variable, %DELFILES%, and change the definition in the environment as you choose to suit the circumstances. Example:

```
ECHO OFF
: [*] FILEDEL.BAT [*]
ECHO    Enter Choice:
ECHO    1. Delete all Backup Files
ECHO    2. Delete all .TXT Files
ECHO    3. Delete all .WKS Files
INPUT
IF ERRORLEVEL 49 IF NOT ERRORLEVEL 50 SET DELFILES="*.BAK"
IF ERRORLEVEL 50 IF NOT ERRORLEVEL 51 SET DELFILES="*.TXT"
IF ERRORLEVEL 51 IF NOT ERRORLEVEL 52 SET DELFILES="*.WKS"
FOR %%a IN (%DELFILES%) DO ERASE %%a
```

You may also use environment variables in batch files as "flags" to determine whether or not certain actions should be carried out:

```
ECHO OFF
IF %FLAG%="YES" GOTO NEXT
ECHO You have not taken your vitamin today!
ECHO Please take it, then resume.
PAUSE
SET FLAG="YES"
:NEXT
```

This example applies to any task that needs to be carried out once after the computer has booted, as would be the case when the system is turned on at the beginning of the day. FLAG will retain the value of "YES," once set, for the rest of the day, for any later tests by batch files, unless the system is rebooted or another copy of COMMAND.COM is permanently substituted for the one storing the current environment.

115

Calling a Second Copy of COMMAND.COM from Batch Files

When a program is called from a batch file, control returns back to the batch file when that program ends, ordinarily. However, while batch files can call one another, they cannot be nested. When a batch file calls another batch file, control never returns to the previous batch file. Thus:

```
ECHO OFF
ECHO Getting ready to run the second batch file now.
PAUSE
BATCH2
ECHO This line will NOT be called when BATCH2 ends.
```

The reason for this is that the command processor, COMMAND.COM, keeps track of where execution of a batch file ceased when programs are called, but does *not* keep track of its "place" in batch files when another batch file is called. Only one pointer is used, and that pointer is appropriated by the new batch file as soon as it begins execution.

There is a way around this. Instead of calling a second batch file, you can invoke a second copy of COMMAND.COM, which can then run the second batch file and return control back to the first (which will pick up the original batch file exactly where it left off).

The syntax for this is:

```
COMMAND /C command
```

The /C tells DOS to carry out the command specified and then return automatically to the original copy of COMMAND.COM. Of course, *command* can be anything, such as DOS commands like DIR, programs, or other batch files. Example:

```
FOR %%a IN (*.*) DO COMMAND C/ ERASEIT %%a
```

In this example, each time through the loop, a second copy of COMMAND.COM will be called to run the batch file

ERASEIT.BAT. That batch file might use INPUT.COM to ask the operator whether or not that file should really be erased. The name of the file is passed along to the second batch file by means of a replaceable parameter, in this case %%a. (These will be discussed in a moment.)

For this trick to work, COMMAND.COM must be available to DOS. For those using hard disks, this is no problem. However, make sure that your PATH command includes a pointer to the root directory of your hard disk (where COMMAND.COM *must* be in order to boot up), or else copy COMMAND.COM to one of the subdirectories specified for a search by PATH. This latter method would prevent DOS from having to search the root directory when it is looking for other files, since COMMAND.COM may be the only file in the root that you use after boot-up.

Invoking a second copy of COMMAND.COM does require an extra 3,000 bytes or so of memory (as does each additional copy you load), so you may want to avoid nesting too many levels of COMMAND.COM with your batch files. Given these restraints, there is no reason why batch files can't call other batch files which call other batch files still.

Using Replaceable Parameters in Batch Files

The previous example should have piqued your interest in exactly what replaceable parameters are. This book has taken the somewhat unorthodox approach of leaving a discussion of replaceable parameters in batch files for last. Most explanations bring this aspect in too early, when those new to batch files may still be easily confused. At this point, you are familiar with nearly all the special subcommands that can be used in batch files. However, the concept of parameters is a key one.

When you type in the root name of a batch file, you may follow on the same command line a series of additional parameters, separated by spaces. You may type in as many as you can fit on a command line. However, DOS is only equipped to handle ten of them at one time, numbered %0 to %9.

When you press Enter and the batch file commences, DOS

assigns the name of the batch file to the parameter %0, which you might think of as a variable similar to those used in BASIC. A line such as

```
ECHO %0
```

would echo the name of the batch file to the screen. Similarly, the next nine parameters you typed on the command line would be assigned to %1 to %9. If you wanted to erase a series of files with a batch file called KILL.BAT, the file itself could look like this:

```
ECHO OFF
: [*] KILL.BAT [*]
ERASE %1
ERASE %2
ERASE %3
ERASE %4
ERASE %5
ERASE %6
ERASE %7
ERASE %9
```

You could then use KILL.BAT by typing the following line:

```
KILL OLD.BAK MCI.ASC MEMOS.*C:\WP\*.BAK
```

In this case, %1 would be assigned the value OLD.BAK, while %2 would become MCI.ASC, and so forth. Since only four parameters have been typed, %5 through %9 would have null values and no files would be erased. You can use these replaceable parameters in many ways, jsut as you would variables in a BASIC program:

```
ECHO OFF
IF %1==HELP GOTO HELP
IF %1=="" GOTO HELP
IF %2==END GOTO END
ERASE *.*
:HELP
ECHO  You need help, friend.
:END
```

Note that a problem would occur if the user happened to start this particular batch file without entering any parameters. In the third line, *nothing* would be substituted for %1, and nothing does *not* equal the null string (""), so no match would take place. To avoid this problem, we can put the parameter inside quotes, too:

```
IF "%1%"=="" GOTO HELP
```

Then, if no parameter is entered, "" will equal "". The double quotes were used around the parameter just to make what is going on clear. However, any single character can match on both sides of the equals signs:

```
IF X%1==X GOTO HELP
```

In this case, if nothing is entered as a parameter, then X will equal X and the label HELP will be accessed.

- SHIFT. This is the final batch file subcommand, saved until now because it is of use only with replaceable parameters. SHIFT causes each parameter typed in on the command line to move over one place to the left (toward %1). So, %2 becomes %1, %3 becomes %2, and so forth. %0 always keeps its identity as the batch file name.

SHIFT has two effects. First, it allows you to type more than nine parameters on a command line. You could type 18 or so short parameters, have the batch file operate with nine of them, and then shift over (invoking SHIFT nine times) and work on the next nine.

In practice, only the second effect of SHIFT is of use: sequentially moving each of the parameters over to become %1 in turn. Our KILL.BAT example could be made much more effective as follows:

```
ECHO OFF
: [*] KILL.BAT [*]
```

```
:ERASE
ERASE %1
SHIFT
IF NOT "%1"=="" GOTO ERASE
```

Now we can type as many file names as can fit on a command line, and the batch file will move each one in turn to parameter %1 and erase it.

Replaceable parameters can call labels, if necessary:

```
ECHO OFF
IF NOT "%1"=="" GOTO %1
:HELP
ECHO Help is on the way.
GOTO END
:ERASE
ERASE *.*
GOTO END
:DIR
DIR A:
GOTO END
:END
```

In this example, you could type the label name on the command line when summoning the batch file. If no label name was typed as a parameter, HELP would be shown. However, if a name that did *not* correspond to a label was entered, the "Label not found" error message would result. For this reason, the user must be very familiar with the input expected for a batch file so that an allowable label is supplied.

Note that in this example, the case of the parameter as typed from the DOS command line does not matter, since DOS automatically converts to uppercase for you in interpreting the parameter as a label name. So you could type "help" or "HELP" or even "HeLp" as a parameter. The value of %1 would be considered as if it were HELP in all three instances, and thus would direct control to the proper label.

This is *not* true within the batch file. You must include tests for all possible combinations of upper- and lowercase characters if you want to be perfectly safe:

```
ECHO OFF
IF "%1"=="YES" GOTO ROUTINE
```

```
IF "%1"=="yes" GOTO ROUTINE
IF "%1"=="Yes" GOTO ROUTINE
IF "%1"=="YEs" GOTO ROUTINE
IF "%1"=="yES" GOTO ROUTINE
IF "%1"=="yeS" GOTO ROUTINE
IF "%1"=="yEs" GOTO ROUTINE
GOTO END
:ROUTINE
ECHO Whew, you said yes.
:END
```

This has been a brief introduction to using batch files to streamline your hard disk operations. In the following chapters, we'll spell out some ways to use the more common DOS commands, and present some specific batch file utilities you can use today to become more productive.

11
More DOS Tricks

Many DOS commands lend themselves to batch file techniques, often because the command itself is rather complex. A simpler batch file command can be substituted. For example, if you have a mental block that keeps you from remembering how to spell CHKDSK, create a batch file called CHECK that incorporates the CHKDSK command. Better yet, avoid learning CHKDSK's syntax by putting together a menu system using INPUT to call each of the various features at the press of a key.

Other DOS commands can be put to work carrying out repetitive functions. Consider the SORT, FIND, and MORE filters. These are special DOS external commands that take ASCII files and other character input and perform some function with them. SORT can be commanded to quickly sort through the file or input and arrange it alphabetically. We can specify the column to sort by, and even sort the same input more than once to arrange the information by several "fields." You can use SORT to rearrange files produced by your own applications.

For example, *Sidekick*'s phone dialer accesses a list of names and phone numbers that you update periodically. The *Sidekick* notepad does include sorting features. However, it might be quicker for some users just to invoke a sorting batch file set up specifically to sort *Sidekick*'s phone file:

```
ECHO OFF
: [*] SORTFON.BAT [*]
TYPE C:\DOS\PHONE | SORT /+4>C:\TEMP.$$$
ERASE C:\DOS\PHONE
COPY C:\TEMP.$$$C:\DOS\PHONE
ERASE C:\TEMP.$$$
```

SORT is a filter, and thus doesn't care exactly how it is fed the information it processes. Thus, there are several ways of directing input to SORT. In this example, we TYPEd the file C:\DOS\PHONE through SORT filter, sorting on the fourth column of the file (+4). In the case of this particular file, the fourth column is where the last name of the person or the name of the corporation begins. The output of SORT is redirected (using ⟩ to a file called TEMP.$$$. Then, the old PHONE file is erased, and the temporary file given its name. The temporary file is then erased. Note that SORT allows a switch—/R—to be placed on its command line to tell it to reverse the sort. Also, SORT can process a file no larger than 63K in size.

FIND is another filter, used to look through ASCII files and locate all the complete lines that either contain, or do *not* contain, a string specified as a parameter for FIND. Syntax is as follows:

```
FIND [switch] [string to find] [filenames to search]
```

When no switch is provided, FIND will search through all the files specified in the file name list to locate the indicated string. Uppercase and lowercase do count. If you use the /V switch, the search will locate only lines that do *not* contain the string. The /C switch tells FIND to display only a count of the number of matching occurrences in the file. The lines themselves are not displayed. This would be useful if you wanted to know roughly how many times a word is used in a file. Only the number of lines in which it is used would be reported, however, not the actual number of times the word was used.

A final switch, /N, tells DOS to display the relative line number of each line that meets the search criteria to be displayed.

Both SORT and FIND allow their output to be redirected to a file, another filter, or a device. For example, you may FIND a string, and then SORT the list of lines containing that string. Or, as shown, you may SORT and direct output to a file.

MORE is another filter; it simply displays the input one screenful at a time, asking the user to press a key to see the next. You could create a batch file called LOOK.BAT along these lines:

```
ECHO OFF
: [*] LOOK.BAT [*]
:LOOK
MORE<%1
SHIFT
IF NOT "%1"=="" GOTO LOOK
```

By typing LOOK FILE1.TXT FILE2.TXT FILE3.TXT, and so forth, on a command line, you could examine a series of ASCII files in convenient pages, one after another.

Redefining Keys

Batch files can be used to redefine your keyboard to suit special needs. We've already talked about device drivers and how ANSI.SYS is a special driver supplied with MS-DOS to allow greater control over the keyboard and screen. One of the things ANSI.SYS does is substitute for the keyboard driver routine built into your IBM PC. Ordinarily, when you press, say, the shifted letter *A*, the keyboard sends the scan code 65 to DOS, which passes it along unchanged. DOS and your applications see the letter *A*. ANSI.SYS usually does the same. However, there are special codes that can be sent to ANSI.SYS to tell it to substitute some other letter, or even a whole string of letters for the one pressed. You might press Alt-A, for example, and instead of passing along Alt-A, ANSI.SYS will send out the string "DIR A: /P." To COMMAND.COM, it looks the same as if you had typed DIR A: /P from the keyboard.

Thus, we can redefine the keyboard to suit our own ends. The process is easy in theory. We need only to send ANSI.SYS a command consisting of the escape character, a left bracket, the scan code of the key to be redefined, and the new definition for that key (which can be either another scan code or a string of characters). The redefinition must end in a lowercase *p*, or 13*p* if the new definition is to end with a carriage return. Examples:

```
ESC[65;97p          turns uppercase A into a
ESC[66;"DIR B:";13p changes B into DIR B: plus
carriage return.
```

Of course, we may *need* A and *a* to be represented properly, and we know a lot of words and DOS commands that require the letter *B*. However, there are many Alt key combinations that can be used and lend themselves readily to key redefinition.

The major problem we run into is that when you press Esc from the keyboard, DOS tends to escape from whatever you were doing. Entering Esc by holding down Alt and typing in 27 (the ASCII code for Esc) does no good: when you are finished, DOS acts exactly as if you had pressed the Esc key.

Fortunately, the PROMPT command has a set of *metastrings* that can be used to send ANSI.SYS messages that can't be typed in easily from the keyboard. These metastrings all consist of a dollar sign ($) and one other character. If the metastring is a dollar sign, plus any of most of the ASCII characters, the string is considered null, and is ignored. For example, $C would be a null metastring.

Because you may want to use some of the metastrings for other purposes, they are all listed here:

$t—the time
$d—the date
$p—the directory of the default drive
$v—the DOS version number
$n—the default drive name
$g—the greater than symbol
$l—the less than symbol
$b—a vertical bar
$q—the equals sign
$h—backspace
$e—Escape
$_—(the underscore) go to the next line on the screen

MORE DOS TRICKS

Note that when a lowercase letter is specified, it *must* be used. $H and $h are *not* the same. For key redefinition, the metastring $e is crucial, because it provides an easy way to send ANSI.SYS the escape character. Just include PROMPT $e in your batch file. You can then follow the $e with whatever string is needed to redefine the key.

In redefining keys, the entire scan code, including the leading 0 used with keys like the Alt combinations, must be put in the definition. Here is an example of key redefinition, You can look up scan codes in Appendix A and make substitutions of your own. Keep in mind that DOS allows only about 200 bytes for new key definitions. If you try to use more space, you may encroach on COMMAND.COM, which is never a good idea when using DOS.

Some special versions of ANSI.SYS that have been patched by dedicated computer maniacs, as well as alternate keyboard drivers may allow longer key redefinitions. You can also use special keyboard macro programs like *Keyworks* or *SuperKey* to produce definitions as long as you like.

However, for our uses, 200 characters are plenty. DIRKEY can be used as a model for your own redefinitions.

```
ECHO ON
:     [*] DIRKEY.BAT [*]
: === Redefines Keys Alt-A to Alt-D ===
ECHO  This file redefines the function keys
ECHO     Alt-A through Alt-D. You may sub
ECHO     stitute definitions of your own for
ECHO     those in quotes. Consult the
ECHO     list of scan codes to use different
ECHO     keys than the ones listed.
ECHO  <alt-255>
ECHO     Hit Control-C to Abort
ECHO  PAUSE
PROMPT $e[0;30;"DIR A:";13p
PROMPT $e[0;48;"DIR B:";13p
PROMPT $e[0;46;"DIR C:";13p
PROMPT $e[0;32;"DIR D:";13p
PROMPT
```

You can redefine keys as you please. Probably the Alt key combinations are the safest to use, since control keys (like Control-C) are used by DOS and many programs. If your application uses ANSI.SYS for its keyboard routines, you'll find that the keys you redefine can be used to provide *macros* within those programs as well.

The function keys can be redefined, of course. Keep in mind that some function keys, such as F1, F2, F3, etc., already have functions defined by DOS. You may not want to preempt those functions—but then again you might.

One problem with redefining keys is that unless the new key definitions are clearly labeled, other users of your computer will be unable to access them. It may be a good idea to standardize within an office on some of the key redefinitions used in common by all workers.

Redefining the System Prompt

Of course, the key purpose for the PROMPT command is *not* to send escape codes to ANSI.SYS. PROMPT was intended as a way of setting the environment variable PROMPT to equal the prompt desired. The metastrings were included as a way of incorporating *variables* into the prompt.

For example, it would do little good to define PROMPT as C⟩. That could be done with the command:

```
SET PROMPT=C>
```

Or just:

```
PROMPT=C>
```

Try it. Now, log over to A:. What happened? Your prompt is *still* C⟩ and not A⟩. The solution is to define the prompt as a variable that DOS will substitute for the correct value dynamically. The most common setting for the prompt, the default definition, is ng, which are the metastrings for the current default drive and the greater than symbol. This prompt will change from A⟩ to B⟩ to C⟩ as required, automatically.

If you scan the list of metastrings, you'll see that we actually have some interesting options for new system

MORE DOS TRICKS

prompts. We can include the current day and date as part of the prompt, as well as the current directory path, DOS version number: lots of different things.

You can choose a new prompt to suit you, and then incorporate a PROMPT statement in your AUTOEXEC.BAT file to make it your new default. Many people like to display the current directory path at all times as a reminder of exactly which subdirectory they are logged onto at the time.

The only drawback to these new prompts is that a prompt can get so long that it fills up most of the line. No problem. Just insert the $_ (underscore) character to move the cursor down to the next line. You can have a two-line prompt, with, say, the second line consisting of the familiar ng prompt you are used to.

But wait, as they say, there's more. Good old ANSI.SYS has many other features we can put to use. One of these allows you to move the cursor around the screen from DOS by means of yet another set of escape codes. PROMPT can be used here to *send* the escape codes to ANSI.SYS at the same time you are redefining the prompt to *include* those escape codes. Here is a typical system prompt used by many hard disk owners:

```
PROMPT=$e[s$e[2;53H$p$e[1;53H$t$h$h$h$h$h$h $d$e[u$n$g
```

This prompt displays the current date and time and directory path in the upper right-hand corner of the screen, and the familiar ng prompt in its usual location elsewhere on the screen. How is this accomplished? First review the cursor movement commands allowed by ANSI.SYS. We'll use the $e to represent escape, but in truth any means you may have of conveying the escape character to ANSI.SYS (through, say, DEBUG) will work.

- $e[s—This string, the first one in the example, saves current cursor position.
- $e[u—Restores cursor to the value it had when the sequence was carried out. This one is used as the third from the last sequence in the example, to restore the cursor to its original position before printing the ng prompt.

- $e[*row;col*H—Instead of *row* and *col*, substitute the row and column you want the cursor to move to for *row* and *col*. In the example, the cursor is moved to row 2, column 53 on the screen, where the directory path of the default drive ($p) is displayed. If you do not specify row and column, the cursor is moved to the home position.

  The cursor is then moved up to the first row, column 53, where the current time is displayed ($t, followed by six backspaces, $h, to erase the seconds and hundredths from the display). A space, the date, $d, are displayed next, whereupon the original cursor position is restored and the ng prompt printed.

Other allowable cursor movement sequences:

- $e[*lines*A—Moves cursor up *lines* rows.
- $e[*lines*B—Moves cursor down *lines* rows. In both these cases, the column in which the cursor appears remains unchanged.
- $e[*columns*C—Moves cursor *columns* positions forward. Default is one; this sequence is ignored if the cursor is already at the far right of the screen; in other words, there is no wrap-around to the next line.
- $e[*columns*D—Moves cursor *columns* positions backward. The default and lack of wrap-around is identical to the preceding sequence.
- $e[*row;col*f—Same as $e[*row,col*H.

More tricks will be presented later in this book. For now, let's put some of these concepts to work with some utitlity programs.

12
Batch File Utilities

This chapter contains a number of utilities putting the batch file programming techniques discussed earlier to work. They will allow you to carry out many hard disk tasks more quickly and efficiently. Most of them illustrate various tricks you can incorporate into your own files. These are by no means the only hard disk shortcuts you can take using batch files.

These examples include prompted file purging, a directory utility, a "safer" way of formatting disks, and faster ways of performing other useful functions. As you are well aware by now, you can summon any of these batch files at any time from the DOS prompt if you (1) have copied them all into a subdirectory (such as one called C:\BATCHES) and (2) have "pointed" DOS in the right direction by incorporating a proper PATH statement in your AUTOEXEC.BAT file. For example, if they are stored in C:\BATCHES, you would include a line like this one:

```
PATH=C:\BATCHES;C:\
```

Include any other subdirectories you want, separating them with semicolons. Review chapter 8 if you are unclear about this.

Purging Files Interactively

MS-DOS lacks a good PURGE command that operates like those found in some other operating systems. While you may delete files using wildcards, there is no easy way to safeguard against accidentally erasing a file you'd like to keep. The most common procedure is first to do a DIR using the wildcard specification, and then manually scan down the list of files presented before retyping the command as ERASE.

Here's a quick shortcut: type DIR *filespecification,* then, after scanning the list, press the cursor pad right arrow key twice. The first two letters of your previous command, DI, will be redisplayed on the screen. You can then type over the *I* with an *E* and press the right arrow key again to dislay the *R* which you can overtype with an *L*. Assuming that the display of files to be deleted is satisfactory, you can immediately press F3 to display the rest of the command you had typed, and Enter to DEL the files with the same specification. This is not only faster, but safer, since you cannot accidentally type in a different file specification by mistake. Or . . . create a batch file:

```
ECHO OFF
: [*] ERASER.BAT [*]
DIR %1
ECHO If you want to delete these files,
ECHO press a key. Otherwise, press Control-C to abort.
PAUSE
ERASE %1
```

Even better would be to use INPUT.COM to *ask* the user to reply "Y" or "N" before deleting the files, to be absolutely certain. You've probably learned enough from this book so far to do that on your own.

But the best solution of all is to show the user each file name, one after another, and ask for confirmation before that file. This would allow browsing through an entire directory and making individual decisions on which files to delete. The following utility tandem, PURGE.BAT and PURGER.BAT, are used together to provide such prompted file deleting. This is a quick way to clean up subdirectories without having to type file names with wildcards (and risk erasing the wrong file) or needing to type individual file names.

To use the utility, type PURGE [d:] [filename], where d: is the optional drive specification and [filename] is the file specification (including wildcards) of the file(s) you want to purge. If you do not specify a drive or directory path, the utility will assume you mean the currently logged drive and directory.

For example, if you are logged onto C:\WP and want to purge files ending in the .TXT extension, you would type:

    PURGE *.TXT

or:

    PURGE C:\WP*.TXT

To purge from a list of *all* files in a directory, just use the *.* global file name:

    PURGE*.*

To file PURGE.BAT, like all the utility files in this book, first check to make sure that a parameter has been entered following the root file name. If not, HELP is presented.

No check is made to see that the parameter, %1, is a valid file specification. Putting comprehensive error traps to catch faulty user input is somewhat clumsy in batch files. DOS will stop file execution just fine if a gross error is made. In most cases, however, you'll need to learn a modicum of syntax (either from this book or from the HELP screens) to use the utilities without crashing them.

Next, the file checks to see if a file called C:\PURGE.$$$ already exists. If so, it is erased. This file is used as a "flag" to tell the batch program whether or not the user has asked to quit. You'll see why in a moment.

The main work of this first batch file is carried out in the next line, where a FOR...IN...DO loop takes each file name specified by %1, and in turn replaces the variable %%a with that file name. Each time through the loop, as long as

C:\PURGE.$$$ has not been created, the batch file summons a second command processor to run the accompanying batch file, PURGER.BAT. Note that variable %%a is passed to PURGER.BAT and becomes the %1 parameter for that batch file.

PURGER.BAT does nothing more than display the file name represented by %1, ask if it should be purged, and then collect the response through INPUT.COM. The answer is tested to see if Y, N, or Q (upper- or lowercase) have been entered. If Q has been pressed, PURGE.$$$ is created, thus aborting further steps after returning to PURGE.BAT. If yes is indicated, the file is erased. Otherwise, it is left alone. When PURGER.BAT ends, the secondary command processor returns control to the first, and PURGE.BAT resumes at the point it left off.

```
ECHO OFF
:       [*] PURGE.BAT [*]
: === Prompted file purging ===
IF "%1"=="" GOTO HELP
IF EXIST C:\PURGE.$$$ ERASE C:\PURGE.$$$
FOR %%a IN (%1) DO IF NOT EXIST C:\PURGE.$$$
   COMMAND /C PURGER %%a
GOTO END
:HELP
ECHO      Type PURGER [d:][filename.ext].
ECHO      You will be asked if you want to delete that
ECHO      file, or individual files that meet the
ECHO      specification. Wildcards are permitted.
ECHO      Substitute drive specification for [d:].
ECHO      <alt-255>
:END
CLS

ECHO OFF
:       [*] PURGER.BAT [*]
: === File purger ===
ECHO %1
ECHO "Purge it? (Y/N/Q)"
:INPUT
INPUT
IF ERRORLEVEL 78 IF NOT ERRORLEVEL 79 GOTO RETURN
IF ERRORLEVEL 81 IF NOT ERRORLEVEL 82 GOTO QUIT
IF ERRORLEVEL 89 IF NOT ERRORLEVEL 90 GOTO PURGEIT
IF ERRORLEVEL 110 IF NOT ERRORLEVEL 111 GOTO RETURN
IF ERRORLEVEL 113 IF NOT ERRORLEVEL 114 GOTO QUIT
IF ERRORLEVEL 121 IF NOT ERRORLEVEL 122 GOTO PURGEIT
GOTO INPUT
```

```
:PURGEIT
ERASE %1
ECHO Erasing your file %1
GOTO RETURN
:QUIT
ECHO QUIT>C:\PURGE.$$$
:RETURN
```

A Sample Menu Utility

Menus provide a quick way of learning to use a utility or application, and of reminding someone who hasn't used the module for a while how it works. For complex commands, a menu can keep the user from scurrying to a manual every time the command is used.

You can build new DOS commands that will allow you to carry out a choice of options from a menu. Thus, the user does not have to remember command syntax—only the root name of the utility. DIRS.BAT demonstrates a simple menu program, providing the user with a choice of eight different directory utilities, including a list of subdirectories in the current directory, files only (no subdirectories), a list of files in all the directories, as well as sorted directories. To use many of the utilities in this chapter, you must have DOS filters, like SORT, FIND, and MORE residing in a subdirectory with a PATH command pointing to them.

In this case, the functions are as follows:

- FILES. Displays files only, redirecting the output of DIR through the FIND filter with the /V switch used to exclude those file names containing the 〈 character. Since the less than symbol is illegal in file names, but used to mark directories 〈DIR〉, this command will automatically isolate the actual file names from the directory names in a given directory.
- SUBS. Shows subdirectories only, using the FIND filter to locate files that *do* include the 〈DIR〉 specification.
- ALL. Shows all files on a hard disk meeting the file specification %1. When CHKDSK is used with the /V switch,

it will display a list of all files on the disk matching the specification. This module redirects that output to SORT, which alphabetizes it and directs it to a temporary file, TEMP.$$$. Then, lines containing the word "Directory" are sent from TEMP.$$$ to a new file named SORTED, and file names containing a backslash but *not* the word "Directory" are sent to file SORTED.

Then, the temporary file is erased and the MORE filter used to display the sorted list of file names meeting the file specification typed in as %1.

- NAME. Sorts directory by file name and displays with pauses between pages.
- SIZE. Sorts directory by file size and displays with pauses between pages.
- DATE. Sorts directory by the date that the file was last updated.
- WIDE. Shows the directory wide, with pauses.
- TEXT. Redirects directory to an ASCII file, FILE.TXT, for examination later using a word-processing program.

```
:        [*] DIRS.BAT [*]
:    === Directory Utilities ===
ECHO OFF
CLS
ECHO  ===== Directory Utilities ====
ECHO       Enter Choice:
ECHO    1. List of Subdirectories in Current Directory.
ECHO    2. List of Files Only in Current Directory.
ECHO    3. List of all files in ALL Directories.
ECHO    4. Directory sorted by Name.
ECHO    5. Directory sorted by Size.
ECHO    6. Directory sorted by Date.
ECHO    7. Directory wide with pauses.
ECHO    8. Store current directory in FILE.TXT.
ECHO    X  EXIT
:INPUT
INPUT
IF ERRORLEVEL 49 IF NOT ERRORLEVEL 50 GOTO SUBS
IF ERRORLEVEL 50 IF NOT ERRORLEVEL 51 GOTO FILES
IF ERRORLEVEL 51 IF NOT ERRORLEVEL 52 GOTO ALL
IF ERRORLEVEL 52 IF NOT ERRORLEVEL 53 GOTO NAME
IF ERRORLEVEL 53 IF NOT ERRORLEVEL 54 GOTO SIZE
IF ERRORLEVEL 54 IF NOT ERRORLEVEL 55 GOTO DATE
IF ERRORLEVEL 55 IF NOT ERRORLEVEL 56 GOTO WIDE
IF ERRORLEVEL 56 IF NOT ERRORLEVEL 57 GOTO TEXT
```

```
IF ERRORLEVEL 120 IF NOT ERRORLEVEL 121 GOTO END
IF ERRORLEVEL 88 IF NOT ERRORLEVEL 89 GOTO END
GOTO INPUT
ECHO OFF
:FILES
: == Shows Files Only ==
DIR | FIND /V "<"
GOTO START
:SUBS
: == Shows Subdirectories Only ==
DIR %1 | FIND "<DIR>"
GOTO START
:ALL
: == Shows All Files ==
CHKDSK %1: /V | SORT > TEMP.$$$
FIND "Directory" TEMP.$$$>SORTED
FIND "\" TEMP.$$$ | FIND /V "Directory" >> SORTED
ERASE TEMP.$$$
MORE < SORTED
GOTO START
:NAME
: == Sort Directory by File Name ==
DIR | FIND /V "Directory" | SORT | MORE
GOTO START
:SIZE
: == Sort Directory by File Size ==
DIR | FIND /V "Directory" | SORT/+14 | MORE
GOTO START
:DATE
: == Sort Directory by Date ==
DIR | FIND /V "Directory" | SORT /+23 | MORE
GOTO START
:WIDE
: == Show Directory Wide, with Pauses ==
DIR /W /P
GOTO START
:TEXT
DIR >FILE.TXT
:START
PAUSE
DIRS
:END
```

REVERSE.BAT

This is an example of a specialized utility. You can create these on the spur of the moment to suit a need that arises. This particular utility, REVERSE.BAT, locates file names that do *not* incorporate a specified string. For example, if you wanted to display a directory of all files *except* those ending in .TXT, you could type:

```
REVERSE TXT
```

You must use uppercase letters. If you follow the string with a drive letter and/or path name, the utility will look in a directory other than the currently logged directory.

```
:           [*] REVERSE.BAT [*]
:           === Locates file names not using specified string ===
IF "%1" == "" GOTO HELP
DIR %2 | FIND /V "%1"
GOTO END
:HELP
ECHO       Locates files without the specified
ECHO          string included in the file name, within the
ECHO          currently logged directory and drive.
ECHO          Use only uppercase characters.
ECHO          Syntax:
ECHO          REVERSE [string] [d:]
ECHO          Note: if other than current directory
ECHO          on logged drive to be used, follow string
ECHO          with full desired pathname.
ECHO          Example: REVERSE TXT C:\WP
ECHO          <alt-255>
:END
```

Failsafe FORMAT

Each successive release of MS-DOS following DOS 2.0 has made it harder and harder to accidentally format your hard disk (early versions of DOS would format the default drive without even checking with you). With DOS 3.2, the need to enter the disk volume label, if one exists, before reformatting a hard disk was introduced. In the future, it may be necessary to enter a password or your mother's maiden name.

However, for those who have versions of DOS before 3.2, this batch file will take some of the worry out of being careless. To use it, you must rename FORMAT.COM to XFORMAT.COM. Once this is done, you may use a batch file called FORMAT.BAT, since FORMAT.COM is an *external* DOS command and only supplants a batch file with the same root name because the .COM extension stands at a loftier level on the systems file hierarchy.

Once you have renamed FORMAT.COM to XFORMAT.COM, you may type FORMAT A: or FORMAT B: as before. However, if you type FORMAT C: with no drive specifier, a stern warning will alert you before possible damage is done.

```
ECHO OFF
:       [*] FORMAT.BAT [*]
: === Anti-Hard Disk Drive Formatter ===
IF "%1"=="" GOTO HELP
IF "%1" == "B:" GOTO B
IF "%1" == "b:" GOTO B
IF "%1" == "A:" GOTO A
IF "%1" == "a:" GOTO A
IF "%1" == "C:" GOTO C
IF "%1" == "c:" GOTO C
GOTO END
:HELP
ECHO   You cannot format the default drive.
ECHO   You must specify drive name explicitly.
GOTO END
:A
XFORMAT A: %2 %3
GOTO END
:B
XFORMAT B: %2 %3
GOTO END
:C
ECHO <alt-7>
ECHO ATTENTION!!!!!
ECHO ==========================================
ECHO You have asked to format your HARD DISK!
ECHO ==========================================
ECHO     Do You Want to Proceed?
ECHO   ENTER "H" TO PROCEED WITH FORMAT OF
ECHO   HARD DISK. ALL DATA WILL BE LOST.
ECHO ==========================================
INPUT
IF ERRORLEVEL 104 IF NOT ERRORLEVEL 105 GOTO HARD
IF ERRORLEVEL 72 IF NOT ERRORLEVEL 73 GOTO HARD
GOTO END
:HARD
XFORMAT C: %2 %3
:END
CLS
```

Prompted File Copying

This utility is similar to the PURGE pair of files presented earlier in the chapter. Instead of erasing files, this one allows you to copy files from one drive and directory to a second drive and/or directory. It takes the form:

```
DUPE [d1:] [filename.ext] [destination d2:]
```

For [d1:] substitute the drive and path name of the file to be copied. If you leave this specification off, the utility will default to the currently logged drive and directory. For [filename.ext] substitute the name of the file you want to copy, using wildcards if necessary to include more than one file. Replace [destination d2:] with the drive and/or path that the new file is to be copied to. You may also specify a new name for the destination file. Examples:

```
DUPE A:*.DOC C:\WP\ARCHIVE
DUPE *.TXT ARCHIVE\*.ARC
DUPE C:\WP\*.* A:

ECHO OFF
:       [*] DUPE.BAT [*]
: === Prompted file copying ===
IF "%1"=="" GOTO HELP
IF "%2"=="" GOTO HELP2
IF EXIST C:\DUPE.$$$ ERASE C:\DUPE.$$$
FOR %%a IN (%1) DO IF NOT EXIST C:\DUPE.$$$ COMMAND /C
DUPER
%%a %2
GOTO END
:HELP
CLS
ECHO     Type DUPE [d1:][filename.ext] [destination d2:].
ECHO       You will be asked if you want to copy that
ECHO       file or individual files that meet the
ECHO       specification. Wildcards are permitted.
ECHO       Substitute source drive specification for [d1:]
ECHO       and destination drive specification for [d2:].
ECHO <alt-255>
GOTO END
:HELP2
ECHO     You MUST specify destination drive and/or
ECHO     directory!!
```

```
ECHO <alt-255>
GOTO HELP
:END
CLS

ECHO OFF
:        [*] DUPER.BAT [*]
: === File Copier ===
ECHO %1
ECHO Copy it? (Y/N/Q)
:INPUT
INPUT
IF ERRORLEVEL 78 IF NOT ERRORLEVEL 79 GOTO RETURN
IF ERRORLEVEL 81 IF NOT ERRORLEVEL 82 GOTO QUIT
IF ERRORLEVEL 89 IF NOT ERRORLEVEL 90 GOTO COPYIT
IF ERRORLEVEL 110 IF NOT ERRORLEVEL 111 GOTO RETURN
IF ERRORLEVEL 113 IF NOT ERRORLEVEL 114 GOTO QUIT
IF ERRORLEVEL 121 IF NOT ERRORLEVEL 122 GOTO COPYIT
GOTO INPUT
:COPYIT
COPY %1 %2
ECHO Copying your file %1 to %2
GOTO RETURN
:QUIT
ECHO QUIT>C:\DUPE.$$$
:RETURN
```

Comparing Contents of Disks or Directories

Subdirectories in hard disks may become cluttered with duplicate files. You may want to check a given backup floppy disk to make sure that you have copied certain files over for safekeeping. This utility allows you to compare the file names on two drives or directories, and list which files are found on both. It takes the form:

```
COMPARE [d1:] [d2:]
```

Replace [d1:] with the hard disk directory path that you want to compare, and [d2:] with the drive and directory path of the second disk. Examples:

```
COMPARE C:\WP A:\
COMPARE C:\WP\ARCHIVE C:\WP\LETTERS
```

To use this file, you need to create a small file containing only the line CD *without* a carriage return at the end. Do this by typing:

```
COPY CON:CD.ASC<Enter>
CD<space><F6><ENTER>
```

Put this file in your BATCHES, or other subdirectory where the batch files are stored, so that this utility and others can find it. It is used to restore your currently logged directory after it is changed by this utility.

This is accomplished by first storing the name of the current directory in a file, DIR.$$$:

```
CD >C:\DIR.$$$
```

The batch file can then change to whatever directory is needed to carry out its functions. Thereafter, a temporary batch file is created that changes the directory back to the original. The file is assembled by combining the file you created earlier, CD.ASC, with DIR.$$$, which stored the former subdirectory name, in a new file, CHBACK.BAT. Then this batch file is run. This technique can be used in your own batch files whenever subdirectories need to be changed and then restored.

```
ECHO OFF
:       [*] COMPARE.BAT [*]
:       === Lists Common Files ===
IF "%1"=="" GOTO HELP
CLS
CD >C:\DIR.$$$
ECHO    Insert Disk to be Compared in %2
PAUSE
CLS
C:
CD %1
FOR %%b IN (*.*) DO IF EXIST %2:%%b ECHO %%b is on both
   disks.
COPY C:\BATCHES\CD.ASC+C:\DIR.$$$ CHBACK.BAT >NUL
ERASE C:\*.$$$ C:\ERASE.$$$
COPY CHBACK.BAT+ERASE.$$$ CHBACK.BAT >NUL
CHBACK.BAT
:HELP
CLS
```

BATCH FILE UTILITIES

```
ECHO  Compares lists of files to see which appear
ECHO  on your hard disk as well as on specified floppy
ECHO  disk or subdirectory. Syntax is as follows:
ECHO  <alt-255>
ECHO  COMPARE [d1:] [d2:]
ECHO  <alt-255>
ECHO  Replace [d1:] with the hard disk directory path
ECHO  that you want to compare, and [d2:] with
ECHO  drive and directory path of the second disk.
ECHO  <alt-255>
ECHO  EXAMPLE: COMPARE C:\WP A:\
```

Updating Your Hard Disk's DOS

Releases of DOS seem to have a useful life of six to nine months before they are supplanted by a later version with features of use to hard disk owners. Applications programs also go through a similar cycle of revision, usually reaching release numbers of 3.0 or some variation before a whole new name is chosen and the numbering process starts over (versions 4.0 or higher of any software seem to smack of overrefinement).

Updating your hard disk with the new files for DOS or your applications program can be a chore that is repeated two or three times a year, and is not as simple as it appears on the surface. Some modules may work with the new release; some may not. Other users don't copy every available file to their hard disks. For example, you may want to avoid having DEBUG available on the hard disk, making it more difficult for you (or others) to tamper with important files. Rather than copying updated files wholesale to the hard disk, you may want to specify in advance which are to be duplicated. DUPE.BAT presented earlier can be used if you or the user knows which files are to be copied. This sample batch file shows how to build a custom updating utility to bring your DOS up-to-date. It can be adapted to any applications program consisting of multiple program or data files.

As written, the utility will first transfer the new system to C:, and then copy from the disk in A: any files that exist *both* on A: and in the specified directory on the hard disk. If you have two disks (as with the DOS and DOS Supplemental programs), you can run this file twice.

143

Note: You must boot from the new DOS disk for this to work properly. SYS transfers the DOS system in memory, and so must operate under the new DOS. Since the new disk will not have an AUTOEXEC.BAT file to match that on your hard disk, a PATH command will not be in effect to tell DOS where to find UPDATE.BAT. After booting, you can log over to the hard disk and change directories to BATCHES to invoke UPDATE.BAT. Or, if you are using DOS 3.x or later versions, you may type C:\BATCHES\UPDATE from any DOS prompt.

```
ECHO OFF
:        [*] UPDATE.BAT [*]
:        === Updates DOS ===
IF NOT "%1" =="" GOTO HELP
CLS
ECHO     BOOT THE NEW DOS DISK. THEN:
ECHO     Insert new DOS disk in drive A:
ECHO     <alt-255>
ECHO        (Hit Control-C to Cancel)
ECHO     <alt-255>
PAUSE
CLS
A:
CD C:\
SYS C:
COPY COMMAND.COM C:\
FOR %%b IN (*.*) DO IF EXIST C:\DOS\%%b COPY %%b C:\DOS
GOTO END
:HELP
ECHO     Insert your new DOS disk in A:.
ECHO     If your DOS subdirectory is named differently,
ECHO     substitute correct name in this file.
:END
```

Finding Strings in Your ASCII Files

Hard disk users tend to collect a lot of ASCII files on their disks. These can be batch files, word-processing files, BASIC programs stored in ASCII form (with the SAVE "FILENAME.BAS",A option), etc. With so many files available, it is easy to lose one or two, or to forget which file was the one containing the word "SEARCH," for example.

This utility will allow you to search through specified sub-

BATCH FILE UTILITIES

directories and files for strings of your choice. Remember, uppercase or lowercase does count. "Search" is not the same as "SEARCH." You may have to do several look-ups, or else look for an intermediate string. For example, if you type "earch," you will find "Search" as well as "search" (but also "Research"). Syntax is as follows:

```
SEARCH [string] [filespecification]
```

If no file specification is used, all files—ASCII files only—in the current subdirectory will be searched.

```
ECHO OFF
:       [*] SEARCH.BAT [*]
:       === Locates strings in ASCII files ===
IF "%1" == "" GOTO HELP
:LOCATE
IF "%2" == "" GOTO FILES
FOR %%a IN (%2) DO FIND "%1" %%a >>LOCATED
GOTO DISPLAY
:FILES
FOR %%a IN (*.*) DO FIND "%1" %%a >>LOCATED
GOTO DISPLAY
:HELP
ECHO    Type SEARCH [string] [filespecification].
ECHO    If no file specification used, all files
ECHO    will be searched. Searches ASCII files only.
ECHO    <alt-255>
GOTO END
:DISPLAY
MORE<LOCATED
:END
```

Moving Files from One Disk or Directory to Another

Often, it will be desirable to move files from one directory or drive to another, either for archiving or because the file doesn't belong in the directory where it is located. MOVER.BAT will perform this chore for you. It can also write over files that you want to keep if you don't check for duplicate file names on the destination diskette or directory first. If an invalid directory name is used, the new file may assume the name of the directory you specified instead of its proper name.

145

To see why, look at how the file works. The syntax is:

```
MOVER [filename] [newname]
```

Examples would include:

```
MOVER A:*.TXT C:\WP
MOVER C:\WP C:\ARC\*.ARC
```

Now, if no subdirectory named C:\WP existed, each file *.TXT would in turn be copied to a new file, called WP. Only the last would remain on the disk, as each new file replaces the old. Worse, the old files *.TXT would be erased. Be careful when typing this command to make sure the directory exists!

Also, if files already reside on the destination disk with the same file name, they will be overwritten. This utility was written as a quick, useful tool for those who wouldn't frequently make such mistakes. However, it would be fairly easy to turn this into a prompted file-copier-deleter, combining the features of PURGE and DUPE into one utility. The IF EXIST test can be used so that the prompting is done *only* if there is some danger of overwriting an existing file. If you have some need for prompted file moving, try this variation on your own:

```
ECHO OFF
:         [*] MOVER.BAT [*]
: === Moves files between directories ===
IF NOT "%1"=="" GOTO MOVE
:HELP
ECHO      Type MOVER [filename] [newname].
ECHO      File will be copied from old directory
ECHO      to new directory, and then erased from
ECHO      the old directory. The parameter [new
ECHO      name] must include drive, directory, or
ECHO      both, and MAY include new file name.
ECHO      <alt-255>
ECHO      EXAMPLES: MOVER A:*.TXT C:\WP
ECHO                MOVER C:\WP C:\ARC\*.ARC
ECHO      <alt-255>
GOTO END
:MOVE
COPY %1 %2
ERASE %1
:END
```

BATCH FILE UTILITIES

Sort ASCII Files

Mailing lists, phone number lists, and other lists need to be sorted, or alphabetized. This utility, FILESORT.BAT, allows you to specify file names to be sorted on the command line. Wildcards cannot be used: you must explicitly state each file name to be sorted. If you have a list of files that you sort frequently, you could also remove the replaceable parameter used with this file and put in a FOR...IN...DO command to sort each of them in turn. Then, once a week or once a month as required, you could type the FILESORT command and have this chore carried out automatically. Such a custom routine would also allow sorting by columns other than the first in each ASCII file.

```
ECHO OFF
:       [*] FILESORT.BAT [*]:
:       === Sorts ASCII Files ===
IF NOT "%1"=="" GOTO SORTER
:HELP
CLS
ECHO    Enter up to 10 file names to be sorted
ECHO    on the command line. Wildcards are not
ECHO    allowed.
ECHO <alt-255>
GOTO END
:SORTER
SORT < %1 > TEMP.$$$
ERASE %1
REN TEMP.$$$ %1
SHIFT
IF NOT "%1"=="" GOTO SORTER
:END
CLS
```

Creating New Directory Paths in One Step

This utility, NEWPATH.BAT, allows you to create new directory paths simply by typing the utility name and the names of the nested subdirectories you want in the order you want them to appear. Don't use the backslash:

```
NEWPATH WP LETTERS JANUARY
```

147

This would create a new subdirectory, WP, with a subdirectory below that called LETTERS, and one below that called JANUARY. If subdirectory WP already exists, the utility will not try to create a new one by that name, but will instead go on to the next step. This utility automatically changes back to the subdirectory you were logged onto when you started. You could type multiple commands:

```
NEWPATH WP LETTERS JANUARY
NEWPATH WP LETTERS FEBRUARY
NEWPATH WP LETTERS MARCH
NEWPATH WP LETTERS APRIL
```

In such a case, the subdirectories would be created in turn. However, you would probably find it easier just to create the first directory path using NEWPATH, and then to log onto subdirectory LETTERS and create the individual subdirectories below it individually. Or, you could use NEWDIRS.BAT (which follows).

```
ECHO OFF
:       [*] NEWPATH.BAT [*]
: === Creates New Directory Paths ===
IF NOT "%1"=="" GOTO BEGIN
:HELP
CLS
ECHO     On command line, list the names of the
ECHO     subdirectory path you want. This file must
ECHO     be used when logged onto the parent of
ECHO     the new subdirectories.
ECHO <alt-255>
GOTO STOP
:BEGIN
CD >C:\DIR.$$$
:PATHS
IF NOT EXIST %1 GOTO CREATE
CD %1
SHIFT
GOTO PATHS
:CREATE
MD %1
CD %1
SHIFT
IF NOT "%1"=="" GOTO PATHS
:END
CLS
```

BATCH FILE UTILITIES

```
COPY C:\BATCHES\C.ASC+C:\DIR.$$$ CHBACK.BAT >NUL
ERASE C:\*.$$$ C:\ERASE.$$$
COPY CHBACK.BAT+ERASE.$$$ CHBACK.BAT >NUL
CHBACK.BAT
:STOP
```

Creating Subdirectories

This utility allows you to create several new subdirectories within a single parent directory with one command. Type the subdirectory names one after another on the command line. You must be logged onto the parent of the new directories to use this file. For example:

```
NEWDIRS January February March April May June July August
```

This would create eight new subdirectories with the names of the first eight months of the year.

```
ECHO OFF
:       [*] NEWDIRS.BAT [*]
: === Creates New Directories ===
IF NOT "%1"=="" GOTO BEGIN
:HELP
ECHO     On command line, list the names of the
ECHO     subdirectories you want. This file must
ECHO     be used when logged onto the parent of
ECHO     the new subdirectories.
ECHO     <alt-255>
GOTO END
:BEGIN
MD %1
SHIFT
IF NOT "%1"=="" GOTO BEGIN
:END
```

Erasing All Files and Removing Subdirectory Path

Removing subdirectory paths can be time-consuming, because DOS will not let you ERASE or DELete a subdirectory itself, only the files in that subdirectory. Directories themselves can be removed only with the RMDIR, or RD, command. To scrap

149

an entire directory path, you must first delete the files in the lowest subdirectory, remove that subdirectory, change to the next highest subdirectory, and repeat the process.

No more. This utility will do all that for you. As a bonus, you *don't* have to type "Y" after each *.* because that is taken care of for you. Here's how the utility works.

To invoke DIRDEL.BAT, type:

```
DIRDEL [directory path to be scrapped]
```

The directory path may include the root directory as the first directory in the path. The utility uses the First, the "Y" needed to answer the "Are you sure?" prompt is put in a file called Y.$$$ on the root directory. Next, the lowest directory in the path specified is logged onto. At this point, a list of files in that subdirectory is displayed, and the user is allowed the opportunity to enter Y, N, or Q, for Yes, No, or Quit. If Y is entered, all the files in that directory are erased, with the file Y.$$$ supplying input to the "Are you sure?" prompt.

After that, the current directory is stored in DIR.$$$, and a CD .. command moves up to the next higher directory in the path. An ASCII file, which you must create prior to using this utility, RD.ASC, is combined with the directory and used to create a file KILLIT.BAT.

RD consists of the characters RD, plus a space, and no carriage return. Create this using COPY CON:

```
COPY CON:RD.ASC<Enter>
RD<space><F6><Enter>
```

A second copy of COMMAND.COM is called to run KILLIT.BAT, thereby removing the subdirectory. The whole process repeats as many times as necessary to trash the entire subdirectory path. The utility repeats until it detects the presence of STOP.$$$, thereby indicating that the root directory, or the directory from which the command was invoked, has been reached. If you should want the process to stop early, create a file called STOP.$$$ in the subdirectory where the utility should cease.

BATCH FILE UTILITIES

```
ECHO OFF
:       DIRDEL.BAT
: === Removes All Files in Nested Subdirectories ===
IF "%1"=="" GOTO HELP
ECHO Y>C:\Y.$$$
C:
ECHO STOP>STOP.$$$
CD %1
:BEGIN
DIR
ECHO   Erase all files in this directory?
ECHO          Y/N/Q?
:INPUT
INPUT
IF ERRORLEVEL 78 IF NOT ERRORLEVEL 79 GOTO NEXT
IF ERRORLEVEL 81 IF NOT ERRORLEVEL 83 GOTO END
IF ERRORLEVEL 89 IF NOT ERRORLEVEL 90 GOTO PURGEIT
IF ERRORLEVEL 110 IF NOT ERRORLEVEL 111 GOTO NEXT
IF ERRORLEVEL 113 IF NOT ERRORLEVEL 114 GOTO END
IF ERRORLEVEL 121 IF NOT ERRORLEVEL 122 GOTO PURGEIT
GOTO INPUT
:NEXT
CD >C:\DIR.$$$
CD ..
COPY RD.ASC+DIR.$$$>KILLIT.BAT
COMMAND /C KILLIT
IF EXIST STOP.$$$ GOTO END
GOTO BEGIN
:PURGEIT
ERASE *.*<C:\Y.$$$
GOTO NEXT
:HELP
CLS
ECHO   Erases all files in a given directory path.
ECHO   Type DIRDEL [last directory].
ECHO   Where [last directory] is the last directory
ECHO   in the path.
ECHO   You will be asked whether to purge each
ECHO   directory.
:END
ERASE STOP.$$$
ERASE C:\*.$$$
```

Deleting Duplicate Files

Where COMPARE.BAT allows you to find out which files are duplicated in two subdirectories, UNDUPE.BAT lets you find and delete the extra copies, automatically. However, you should be sure that any duplicates you find are in fact duplicates and not two different files with the same name. You could add a prompting routine to this, such as found in PURGE.BAT, to let you decide whether or not to kill the duplicate files. You should in any case adopt a unique naming scheme so that files are less likely to have the same name even though they reside in different subdirectories.

The syntax for this utility is as follows:

```
UNDUPE [d1:] [d2:]
```

Replace [d1:] with first path name, and [d2:] with second drive\path name. Files found in both will be erased from [d2:]. Examples:

```
UNDUPE C:\WP C:\BAK
UNDUPE C:\FILES\ARCHIVE A:

ECHO OFF
:       [*] UNDUPE.BAT [*]
: === Kills duplicate hard disk files ===
IF "%1"=="" GOTO HELP
C:
CD %1
FOR %%b IN (*.*) DO IF EXIST %2%%b ERASE %2%%b
GOTO END
:HELP
CLS
ECHO    Syntax:
ECHO    UNDUPE [d1:] [d2:]
ECHO    Replace [d1:] with first C:
ECHO    path name, and [d2:] with second
ECHO    drive\path name. Files found in
ECHO    both will be erased from [d2:].
ECHO    EXAMPLE:
ECHO    UNDUPE C:\WP C:\BAK
ECHO    <alt-255>
:END
```

13
Advanced File Management Made Easy

Until recently, lack of information frequently kept managers from making the best decisions in many situations. One hundred and twenty-five years ago, businesses that tried to conduct commerce over a large geographical area found that delays of weeks or months stood between the "home" office and managers in the field. When the telephone, telegraph, and radio made it possible to move information at the speed of light, there was no way to process that information into a form that could be readily used and acted upon.

Now we have computers that can process information and extract reams of data as spreadsheets, reports, memos, graphics, and other forms. Instead of an information gap, we have information overload.

The typical user of a hard disk drive will accumulate a vast quantity of files. These can be difficult to manage if a well-designed file management routine is not used. Otherwise, the user may rapidly become immersed in a situation where all the information needed resides *somewhere* on the hard disk—but there is no good way to find it.

Given the minimum cluster size that can be allocated on a hard disk, a 20-megabyte drive can accumulate as many as 10,000 different files. The actual number is likely to be much less than this: DOS, applications, and subdirectories take up disk capacity, and most files are larger than the minimum size. However, 3,000 files on a 20-megabyte hard disk is not unreasonable—and computers with 40, 60, or 80 megabytes of capacity are becoming more common.

Subdirectories alone are not the key to filing and organizing individual data files. Most users would be hard-pressed to think up 30 different categories for their documents, which could still leave an average of 100 documents per subdirectory.

Another possible solution was mentioned earlier in the book: use file names themselves as a way of differentiating among files. DOE01027.LET, for example, could represent a letter written by Doe on January 2, 1987. We could find all of Doe's correspondence by typing DIR DOE?????.LET, or we could look for January letters with DIR DOE01???.LET, or even search for *all* letters written in January with DIR ???01???.LET.

However, this scheme has drawbacks of its own. There are only eight characters in the file name, plus three in the extension for the coding scheme. As it is, we've allowed only three for the author's name. Some programs, such as Lotus *1-2-3*, require that specific extensions like .WKS be used, preempting more than a quarter of the available coding space. Moreover, it may be necessary to have a decoder ring available by the computer to decipher what codes are used to represent what documents.

The best solution is to combine the two methods, using subdirectories as well as file-naming conventions to produce an efficient document management system. This chapter will describe a typical system on which you can model your own.

Build a Model

The first step is to construct a model of how documents are created and used in your own application. The exact system you implement will depend quite heavily on the number of documents, how they are differentiated, and who needs to access them.

Write down all the different file types that must be managed. Try to be as thorough as possible, and group them together where appropriate. A typical list might look like this:

- Word Processing
    - Letters
        - To Customers
        - To Suppliers
        - To Branch Offices
        - To Media
    - Memos
    - Proposals
        - To Customers
            - First Drafts
            - Revisions
        - Internal
            - First Drafts
            - Revisions
    - Working Notes
    - Misc.
- Spreadsheets
    - Accounts Payable
    - Accounts Receivable
    - General Ledger
    - Taxes
- Database
    - Mailing Lists
    - Customer Files
    - Resources

If your model is going to be the basis for file management for several users, pass this list around for people to add their own document types. Try to think of all the different stages a file goes through from the time it is created through revisions and final versions. You will need a way to "mark" each of these. How would this information be filed if it were in paper form? By year, by geographical area, by company division?

Who will be accessing the information? Do certain sets of documents "belong" to one person? In the case of letters, it is likely that the person writing the letter will be the only one who will need to see it in the future. However, other types of documents, such as customer lists in databases, may be regularly accessed by several users sharing a single computer or secretary.

Lay out the model in the form of a flowchart, if appropriate, or as a hierarchy. From there, the next step is to design "file cabinets" to put each in.

Design Subdirectory File Cabinets

Earlier in this book there was a discussion of laying out a hierarchical subdirectory structure. Much of the groundwork needed for this step was laid out there. In fact, you might have to make only a few modifications to fine-tune the subdirectories you set up at that time.

One change you may want to make will be to add separate subdirectories for years. Many different types of documents can be conveniently grouped by the year in which they were created. So you may have a subdirectory C:\WP within which are directories for each of the most recent years:

```
Directory: C:\WP
    Subdirectories:     1988                        ⟨DIR⟩
        Subdirectories:         LETTERS            ⟨DIR⟩
                                MEMOS              ⟨DIR⟩
                                PROPOSALS          ⟨DIR⟩
                                WORKING NOTES      ⟨DIR⟩
                                MISC.              ⟨DIR⟩
                        1987                        ⟨DIR⟩
        Subdirectories:         LETTERS            ⟨DIR⟩
                                MEMOS              ⟨DIR⟩
                                PROPOSALS          ⟨DIR⟩
                                WORKING NOTES      ⟨DIR⟩
                                MISC.              ⟨DIR⟩
```

To see all letters for 1987, you could type:

```
DIR C:\WP\1987\LETTERS
```

If the batch file that loads your word-processing program first changes the current directory to C:\WP, the task becomes even easier, as only the 1987\LETTERS portion has to be typed when accessing a directory from within the word-processing program. *Tip:* If most of the activity for a certain type of document occurs within the year it is created, store all of *this* year's documents in the parent subdirectory. Previous years' information is deposited in the other subdirectories, so that the current year's files become your defaults:

```
Directory: C:\WP
                  LETTERS              ⟨DIR⟩
                  MEMOS                ⟨DIR⟩
                  PROPOSALS            ⟨DIR⟩
                  WORKING NOTES        ⟨DIR⟩
                  MISC.                ⟨DIR⟩
                  1987                 ⟨DIR⟩
Subdirectories:   LETTERS              ⟨DIR⟩
                  MEMOS                ⟨DIR⟩
                  PROPOSALS            ⟨DIR⟩
                  WORKING NOTES        ⟨DIR⟩
                  MISC.                ⟨DIR⟩
```

Once logged into C:\WP, to see the contents of the 1988 LETTERS subdirectory, just type:

```
DIR LETTERS
```

To see last year's 1987 letters, you would still type:

```
DIR 1987\LETTERS
```

Better yet, instead of calling the subdirectories 1987, etc., why not call them 87, 86, etc.? Or even 6,7? To move a letter from A: to the 1987 letters subdirectory, you would only have to type:

```
COPY A:LETTER.LET C:\WP\7\LETTERS
```

The advantage of setting up a more sophisticated subdirectory structure to store files is that you are not limited to eight or eleven characters for the entire file descriptor. It's best to keep the directory names as short as possible to reduce typing, but they can also be as long as necessary for easy look-up without referring to a key.

Although this course is not recommended, the subdirectory structure can be as sophisticated as necessary to encompass every possible document. Conceivably, you could have a document path name like this:

```
C:\WP\1987\LETTERS\BUSCH\SMITHCO\JUNE\10
```

This particular subdirectory would store all 1987 letters written by Busch to client SMITHCO on June 10. It would take even a neophyte about a minute to learn how to use such a subdirectory structure. However, the time wasted in typing such a long descriptor every time a file is created, stored, or accessed would be costly. Instead, a much less restrictive directory structure can be used, and the file names themselves used to further differentiate documents. The needs of your organization will determine at which point the break needs to be made. With many documents to manage, a larger directory structure may be necessary since file names are, after all, limited in the number of characters. A smaller number of documents may be better served by a simpler directory structure and coding the file names themselves.

Establish File Name Conventions

Using limited-length and fixed-length fields to describe documents has been around much longer than personal computers. Microfilm systems, for example, have been using strings of characters to index and retrieve document images for many years.

The first place to start is with the file name extension. Some applications programs require that the extension be constant: TXT, DOC, BAK, WKS, and so forth are common requirements. If your applications don't preempt the extension, the concepts described in the paragraphs that follow can be extended for even more flexibility.

There are two keys to getting the most from your eight-character limit. First, every descriptor should appear in the same position in the file name every time. Second, you should make every position count. The fewer positions used up needlessly, the more will be available to store descriptive information. Examine a typical file name code:

`DB88P9RS.DOC`

In this case, we'll assume that the extension, .DOC, has been preempted by the word-processing program. The sample file name, which is actually one character longer than it needs to be, contains the following information: the file is a word-processing document created by David Busch in August 1988 as a proposal for the Smithco Company. This is a revision that has been approved and sent.

How was all that information packed in there? The .DOC extension tells us that it is a word-processing document. The first two letters of the file name, DB, are the initials of the author. This works in an organization where no two users have the same initials. Small organizations find it easier to present as much information as possible—or humanly interpretable—without a key, so initials are a handly way of doing this. If more information must be packed into the file name, we'll show you a way in moment of encoding up to 36 different authors using a single position in the file name.

The next position, the first 8, indicates that the document was created in August, the eighth month. What do we do for October, November, and December, the tenth, eleventh, and twelfth months? We *could* have allocated two positions for the month, but this would have been wasteful for information that is needed only 25 percent of the time. Instead, we can let the letter A represent 10, just as it does in the hexadecimal and duodecimal (base 12) numbering systems, while B can represent 11, and C, 12. By using the numbers 1-9 and letters A-C, all 12 months can be represented.

We could also have used 0 for 10, and A for 11, but those who use hexadecimal find the proposed system much easier to remember. For the rest of us, it is no strain to learn to recognize this code.

The next 8 represents the last digit of the year, 1988. There is no need to enter the whole year, or even 88, since it is a rare application in which files going back more than nine years are used. In 1998, we can just dump all the 1988 files, if they are still on-line and begin over.

By this time you may have guessed how we can represent 36 authors by a single character. Just assign each of them a number from 0 to 9, and an alpha character from A to Z. Thirty-six different designators are available, and can be fit into a single position in our file name. You may have to look up who is who from a key chart, but frequent users of a file-naming system soon memorize the important descriptors.

Similarly, 36 different document types can be represented in the same way. If you have only five or ten types, you might try using mnemonics, as P for proposal, L for letters, etc. Other positions in the file name stand for customer or client (36 different names), and status of the document (R for revision, 1 for first draft, F for final draft). The final character can be used to represent a finer degree of status, S for sent, X for rejected, A for approved, etc. With all the information contained in this file name, we actually had two characters to spare. You may use extra characters for your own descriptors or to expand beyond the 36-item limitation.

Most organizations will require a "key" to allow users to find the documents they want by reconstructing the file name from the information at hand. This chart will list all the document types and their codes, author or user codes, basic sub-directory structure, and other information. If you have a memory-resident notepad, this key can be placed there ready for instant access at the press of a hot key. It may simply be more convenient to print out the code and tape it near the computer.

Once a file-naming system has been designed, many tasks can be streamlined through the use of wildcards in the file names. For example, to copy all the letters written by Busch during 1988 to a diskette, just type in the following:

```
COPY C:\WP\8\LETTERS\DB*.DOC A:
```

To find proposals by that same person that have been approved, you might type:

```
DIR C:\WP\DB??P??A.DOC
```

As you see, you can "plug in" information that will describe the files you are looking for in many flexible ways.

Locate Files with a Batch Utility

Sometimes, through an operator error, files get mislaid. You may accidentally copy them to the wrong subdirectory or provide them with a name that is slightly wrong (using your file-naming scheme).

Fortunately, DOS has a way of listing every file on the disk, using the CHKDSK utility. If you type:

```
CHKDSK C: /V
```

DOS will display a list of every file on the hard disk. It is usually more useful to redirect the output of CHKDSK to a file, so that the information can be scanned, using the MORE filter to display the file in pages, or by means of a word processor that allows import of ASCII text. The word-processing program has the advantage of allowing you to scroll back and forth within the file, and use global search commands to scan for specific file name strings.

You probably should browse through a CHKDSK listing of your files once a year to look for duplicates and files that are no longer needed. A disk-cataloging utility is a useful addition to many end users' hard disks. Those who don't adopt a complex file name code scheme can use such a utility to locate files on the hard disk, as the mnemonic information that can be recalled is frequently enough to locate the desired file. Those who have a code scheme have less need of a disk-cataloging utility, but such a facility can be useful to locate strayed files, and as a file maintenance tool.

DISKCAT.BAT is a batch file utility that takes care of many file-tracking chores. Its operation is extremely simple. Activate the utility by typing DISKCAT.

Then, you'll be presented with a menu offering three choices:

```
1. Add New Files to a Catalog
2. Locate a File
X  Exit
```

INPUT.COM and the necessary checks are used to reject any user key input other than 1, 2, or X (upper- or lowercase). Of course, as always, the batch file can be aborted by typing Control-C or Control-Break.

If the updating step is required, CHKDSK is invoked and the information stored in a temporary file, TEMP.$$$. Next, that information is scanned using FIND to locate file names with the backslash, which indicates a path name, and that information is stored in the file C:\DISKS. If you wish, you can redirect this through the SORT filter to provide a sorted list of file names, and you can change the C:\DISKS file name to deposit the data file in one of your subdirectories for permanent storage. Be sure and change the name in LOCATE.BAT as well.

If the user chooses to locate a file, the instructions and syntax for using LOCATE.BAT are presented. However, LOCATE.BAT is a stand-alone utility that can be used to access the C:\DISKS data file at any time. The syntax for LOCATE.BAT is:

```
LOCATE [filename or string]
```

You must use uppercase letters. The entire string you are looking for does not have to be entered. FIND will locate all files that contain that string, even partially. Therefore, you might type:

```
LOCATE DOC
LOCATE DB
```

The first command would locate all files ending in DOC, as well as DOCUMENT.WKS and every document in the subdirectory C:\WP\DOCS. The second command would find all files with DB in the file name, such as DB55P9AA.DOC, or FILES.DB, or C:\DBASE\.

```
ECHO OFF
:      [*] DISKCAT.BAT [*]
: === Tracks Hard Disk Files ===
:MENU
ECHO   ===== Disk Cataloger ====
```

ADVANCED FILE MANAGEMENT MADE EASY

```
ECHO         Enter Choice:
ECHO     1. Add New Files to Catalog.
ECHO     2. Locate a File.
ECHO     X  To Exit.
:INPUT
INPUT
IF ERRORLEVEL 49 IF NOT ERRORLEVEL 50 GOTO UPDATE
IF ERRORLEVEL 50 IF NOT ERRORLEVEL 51 GOTO LOCATE
IF ERRORLEVEL 120 IF NOT ERRORLEVEL 121 GOTO END
IF ERRORLEVEL 88 IF NOT ERRORLEVEL 89 GOTO END
GOTO INPUT
:UPDATE
CLS
ECHO    Process will take a few minutes. Please wait.
ECHO    <alt-255>
PAUSE
CHKDSK C: /V > TEMP.$$$
FIND "\" TEMP.$$$> C:DISKS
ERASE TEMP.$$$
GOTO END
:LOCATE
CLS
ECHO Type LOCATE [file string].
ECHO If you can remember only part of file
ECHO name, enter that. USE ALL CAPS.
:END


ECHO OFF
:       [*] LOCATE.BAT [*]
: === Finds Hard Disk Files From Catalog ===
IF "%1"=="" GOTO HELP
CLS
FIND "%1" C:DISKS
GOTO END
:HELP
CLS
ECHO Type LOCATE [file string].
ECHO If you can remember only part of file
ECHO name, enter that. USE ALL CAPS.
:END
```

14
Hard Disk Security

It is fortunate that most microcomputer applications don't require extraordinary security measures to protect programs and data from unauthorized users. Almost all data stored on a hard disk is valuable, if only in terms of the time that was required to capture it or key it in. Some information takes on a special value if it is used to make key decisions in a company, or could be used by competitors. That data must be protected both from tampering and from copying by unauthorized personnel who may gain access to a particular computer. In addition, data must be protected from accidental loss due to a hardware failure. The importance of data backup will be covered later in this book. This chapter deals with protecting the computer from unauthorized users, and includes a novel "lockout" routine that can discourage casual tampering.

But first, face one fact: a determined, knowledgeable computer tamperer can bypass nearly any protection scheme you can devise, particularly one based on software. If your data is *very* important, don't store it in or near the computer at all. Keep the information *only* on removable media like floppy disks, and lock up those diskettes in a safe whenever the computer is not closely supervised by an authorized person. Then your data will be as secure as the safe or integrity of the authorized personnel permits.

It would not be difficult to write a batch file that would

copy key data files to diskettes at the end of the day, and erase them from the hard disk. Another batch file would copy them back to the hard disk for use the next day. It is recommended that two copies to floppy disk be made, and that they be stored in different locations. This method would have the advantage of allowing one worker to use key information on more than one hard-disk-equipped computer over the course of a few days. The disadvantage would be the time required to copy and erase the files each day.

Don't forget that the entire computer can be stolen. There are locking mechanisms that will chain the system unit to a desk, forcing the thief to attempt to make off with the whole desk. Someone equipped with a power screwdriver or a fast wrist can remove the cover of your computer and take out the hard disk or hard disk card in a minute or two. The drive can then be smuggled out in a briefcase much more easily than, say, the entire system unit. Again, there are locks that prevent opening the cover of the machine and lock out the power switch as well.

PC-AT era and later computers frequently are furnished with a key lock that can be used to "secure" the system. However, keys can be duplicated, and not every user will take the time to lock the system when leaving for the water cooler.

It is possible to protect data from unknowledgeable users by burying it deep in a tangled nest of subdirectories and dummy subdirectories. Batch files can be written that allow you to change to the proper directory when necessary to run applications. Menu systems that only allow the user to access certain data without entering a password also provide a modicum of protection. However, it is fairly easy to break out of such menus by pressing Control-C or Control-Break. At the DOS prompt, most users can do what they will with your computer. A hard disk computer can also be booted from any DOS disk the user may bring along.

A Hard Disk Security System

The following system for providing hard disk security is probably the most flexible and sophisticated that you are likely to

HARD DISK SECURITY

see using simple techniques. It has features designed to deter even mildly sophisticated tamperers—although the true computer expert will have no difficulty with it. However, unless it is *your* data that is desired, most gremlins will choose to go on to easier pickings rather than risk messing with your computer. Here's what you need to do:

If you have a PC-XT or PC with two full-height side-by-side drives, *reverse* the position of them, so that A: is on the right and B: is on the left. When you leave the computer unattended, put a DOS bootable disk in the right, A:, drive with an AUTOEXEC.BAT file along these lines:

```
ECHO OFF
:   [*] AUTOEXEC.BAT [*]
:   == Booby-trapped AUTOEXEC.BAT ==
CLS
ECHO ******** UNAUTHORIZED USER !!!! ********
CTTY COM1
:BELL
ECHO <alt-7>
GOTO BELL
```

What may happen is that the thief comes along and finds your computer locked by the system presented later in this chapter. He or she may press Control-Alt-Delete to try and bypass the protection scheme. The thief may even be smart enough to put a DOS disk in the left drive, thinking it is A:. However, the system will boot from the *right* drive, containing the booby-trapped AUTOEXEC.BAT file. It will lock up the keyboard and start the internal speaker beeping. Control-C will stop the sound, but leave the computer locked up. The thief, probably nervous by this time, will have to figure out that the drives have been reversed and put a standard DOS disk in the right-hand drive to defeat the system. But don't count on it.

If you do not want to make this hardware change, or cannot because you have only one disk drive, the LOCK system has another subtle booby trap built into the AUTOEXEC.BAT file on the hard disk, so that no one but you will be able to boot from your hard disk.

Using LOCK

Create a subdirectory on your hard disk called C:\LOCKER. Copy to it the following files:

```
LOCK.BAT
TIMER.BAT
UNLOCKER.BAT
RELEASE.BAT
RELEASE.ASC
SET.ASC
CR.ASC
RETURN.ASC
DATE.ASC
```

The first four are normal batch files. The five .ASC files are simple text files used to build other files while LOCK runs. Note: All the .ASC files should be created using COPY CON:, so that some of them can be built *without* a carriage return at the end of the line. This is needed so that we can combine these files with other information on the same line in the final file. You create a file without a carriage return at the end by typing F6 at the end of the line, before hitting return:

```
COPY CON:SAMPLE.ASC<Enter>
THIS LINE HAS NO C/R<space><F6><Enter>

COPY CON:HAS_CR.ASC<Enter>
THIS LINE HAS A C/R<Enter>
<F6><Enter>
```

Now, test what has been done by typing these lines:

```
COPY SAMPLE.ASC+HAS_CR.ASC ONELINE.ASC
COPY HAS_CR.ASC+SAMPLE.ASC TWOLINES.ASC

TYPE ONELINE.ASC
THIS LINE HAS NO C/R THIS LINE HAS A C/R

TYPE TWOLINES.ASC
THIS LINE HAS A C/R
THIS LINE HAS NO C/R
```

Type in the .ASC files as shown in the listing, putting spaces where ⟨space⟩ is indicated, and pressing the Return or Enter key where ⟨Enter⟩ is indicated and F6 where ⟨F6⟩ is shown. You must follow the instructions exactly for LOCK to work.

There are two other small changes that need to be made to allow the system to function. If you have DOS 3.x with VDISK, you need to add a line in the CONFIG.SYS file creating a virtual disk with at least 15,000 bytes of free memory available. Syntax is as follows:

```
DEVICE=VDISK.SYS 15
```

If you have some other RAM disk program, follow the instructions supplied with it to create a RAM disk called D:. If you have *no* RAM disk software at all, LOCK will still work. Simply delete the lines with COPY in them from LOCK.BAT, along with the line that logs over to D:. The routine will run from your hard disk, but will constantly access the hard disk while the computer is locked. This should not harm your hard disk. However, using the RAM disk eliminates using the hard disk at all while the system is locked, and it is quieter, too.

You should have FIND.EXE on your hard disk in a subdirectory called C:\DOS. If FIND.EXE resides somewhere else, change the LOCK.BAT line that copies it to the RAM disk to reflect the true location. If you are not using a RAM disk, make sure PATH points to where FIND.EXE is located.

LOCK also writes to the environment. Those who insist on using DOS 2.x with a hard disk may not have enough room in their environment. Those with DOS 3.x will want to include a SHELL= statement in their CONFIG.SYS file to expand the environment.

```
SHELL=COMMAND.COM /P/ E:60 (For DOS 3.1)
SHELL=COMMAND.COM /P/ E:960 (For DOS 3.2 and later
versions)
```

Finally, you'll need to put one booby trap in your AUTOEXEC.BAT file as the first few lines. The routine looks like this:

HARD DISK SOLUTIONS WITH BATCH FILE UTILITIES

```
TYPE DATE.ASC
INPUT
IF ERRORLEVEL 64 IF NOT ERRORLEVEL 65 GOTO RIGHT
CTTY COM1
:LOOP
ECHO <alt-7>
GOTO LOOP
:RIGHT
(The rest of your AUTOEXEC.BAT file continues here.)
```

Once this has been done, you are ready to go. Boot the computer from the hard disk. You'll be shown something that looks very much like the "enter date" prompt of DOS for a computer not equipped with a clock card (on a PC-AT this may look odd, but still should not alert the potential thief—yet). However, *don't* enter the date. Instead, you must press F6. If any other key is pressed, the computer will lock up and bells will start beeping from the internal speaker. No matter how many times the thief tries to boot from your hard disk this will happen, unless he or she happens to guess and press F6—or if the perpetrator is *very* quick and presses Control-C before AUTOEXEC.BAT gets to INPUT, or while it waits for INPUT.

If you wanted to, you could add a second INPUT line and require that a second key be pressed before the AUTOEXEC.BAT file continues. However, most thieves will catch on by this time.

LOCK allows setting a time lock on your computer so it will be frozen for a given period. This is safer than a password system, because the computer doesn't have to periodically ask for a password and thereby leave itself open to Control-C tampering. Once you have locked the computer in this way, there is no way to regain control until the time is up without rebooting, and we have already put in some obstacles to block *that*. To lock the computer, type LOCK [time to release], where [time to release] is the system time in hours and minutes you desire, separated by a colon. For example, if it is 12:00 noon, and you want the computer to be locked while you are at lunch, type:

```
LOCK 13:00
```

Note that the 24 hour clock is used. The computer will freeze up and automatically release itself at 13:00. If anyone tries to break out of the routine by typing Control-C, the computer will freeze up for good, until the next reboot. If you are leaving your desk temporarily to go to the water cooler, you can set the delay for a minute, or two, or five, as you prefer. This is all you need to know to use LOCK.

Those who like to pick apart computer programs may be charmed by the rather elaborate techniques used to accomplish this trick, since DOS's batch file language doesn't have any simple way to check for the time and perform some action therefrom. You *can* compare strings, such as variables stored in the environment, and create files, check for the existence of files, and so forth, and that is what was done with this utility. One batch file at a time, here is how the LOCK system works.

LOCK.BAT

This batch file sets the time to release the system and activates the lock as well as the checking routine that looks to compare the current time.

First, the parameter %1 is compared with the null string "" to see if they match. If so, meaning no time was entered by the user, HELP is displayed.

If a time was specified, the environment variable UNLOCK is set to equal "RELEASE : Current time is " plus %1, which will be the time to release the system. The reason why this exact string must be used, rather than just the time to release the system, will become apparent shortly.

Next, the LOCK files, plus FIND.EXE, are copied to D:. The NUL redirection is used to keep the "Files copied" output from being displayed on the screen. (The technique is chiefly shown for illustration: the output won't display in any case because the screen output has been redirected to COM1 by CTTY.) If you are not using a RAM disk, delete these lines and the following one that logs over to D:.

Temporary files with the .$$$ extension are erased. This

is done because LOCK can be used more than once during the day, and the files might still be there from the last use. The presence of one of them is used as a flag to indicate that the lockout routine should end.

The screen is cleared and a message displayed indicating that the computer is locked. Delete this if you do not wish to tip anyone off.

The CTTY COM1 line redirects the standard input and output of the system to the COM1 port, effectively locking out the screen and keyboard from the user. The computer will still respond to Control-C and end the batch file routines, but will not turn control back over to the keyboard and screen.

The next batch file, UNLOCKER.BAT, is called.

UNLOCKER.BAT

Each time this batch file is run, it checks to see if a file called ALARM.$$$ exists. If it does exist, then the time period is up and the file branches to the END label, which unlocks the computer with CTTY CON and chimes a beep to signal the operator.

However, until that happens, the file continues. The next line echos the environment variable %NOW% to a file called NOW.ASC. Variable %NOW% will always contain a string reading: "RELEASE : Current time is hh:mm:ss" with hh:mm:ss replaced by the most recent hours, minutes, and seconds.

Next, FIND is used to compare another environment variable, %UNLOCK%, to see if that string (set to the time for unlocking the computer by LOCK.BAT) can be found in the ASCII file, NOW.ASC. If it can (because the hh:mm in NOW.ASC matches %UNLOCK%, then READY.BAT will contain the string %UNLOCK% (RELEASE : Current time is, etc.). If no match is made, READY.BAT will contain a series of hyphens.

Next, a second command processor is called to run the file that has just been created, READY.BAT. If the time is not up yet, READY.BAT will have the hyphens, and DOS will try to find a hyphen-named system file—unsuccessfully. So, READY.BAT will end there and return control to UNLOCKER.BAT, which then calls TIMER.BAT.

However, if a match *is* made, then READY.BAT will contain the line:

```
RELEASE : Current time is . . . etc.
```

Everything following the colon will be interpreted as an illegal label (ignored) by DOS. However, DOS will first look for a system file with the root name RELEASE, and will find RELEASE.BAT. (Is it becoming clear now why %NOW% has to be constructed as it is?)

RELEASE.BAT does nothing but create ALARM.$$$ using the dummy string "NOW!" Because this file has been created, the next time UNLOCKER.BAT encounters the IF EXIST line, the lock routine will end.

However, that doesn't take place quite yet. In all cases, control returns from the second command processor (which has its own separate environment, therefore precluding putting our flag there, instead of creating ALARM.$$$). TIMER.BAT is run next.

TIMER.BAT

The recursiveness or whatever you choose to call it of this LOCK routine gets a bit hairy right now. Let's take this slow:

The first line of TIMER.BAT invokes the DOS TIME command, and supplies it input from the .ASC file CR.ASC, which contains nothing but a carriage return. This automatically responds to the TIME request for a new time with a carriage return, which keeps the old time. However, the output is redirected to a file called TIME.$$$ through the FIND filter, which looks for "Current" (and therefore filters out the second line output by the TIME command). Got that?

The next line constructs a new batch file, called TIME-NOW.BAT from the contents of SET.ASC, RELEASE.ASC, TIME.$$$ (produced above), and RETURN.ASC.

SET.ASC contains "SET NOW=" without a carriage return, RELEASE.ASC contains "RELEASE :" without a carriage return, and TIME.$$$ contains "Current time is hh:mm:ss" followed by a carriage return. RETURN.ASC has just a single line, "UNLOCKER". File TIMENOW.BAT will look something like this:

```
SET NOW=RELEASE : Current time is 12:13:44.1
UNLOCKER
```

The last line in TIMER.BAT runs the batch file just created, thereby setting the environment variable %NOW% to the current time (plus RELEASE, etc.) and then invoking the batch file UNLOCKER.

Of course, UNLOCKER immediately checks for ALARM.$$$. If it has been created on the last pass through, the lock procedure ends. Otherwise it proceeds until ALARM.$$$ is created.

Simple, no? This routine just proves that amazing things can be programmed with batch files even without decent commands available.

The listings for the batch files and .ASC files follow.

```
ECHO OFF
:   [*] LOCK.BAT [*]
:   == Locks the Computer ==
IF NOT "%1"=="" GOTO LOCK
ECHO To Set Time to unlock computer, type: LOCK [hh:mm].
ECHO Where hh=hours (include leading zeros).
ECHO Where mm=minutes (include leading zeros).
ECHO Separate with colon.
ECHO EXAMPLE:
ECHO        LOCK 12:15
ECHO .
GOTO END
:LOCK
SET UNLOCK=RELEASE  : Current time is %1
COPY C:\LOCKER\*.* D: >NUL
COPY C:\DOS\FIND.EXE D: >NUL
D:
ERASE *.$$$
CLS
ECHO *=======================================*
ECHO *          COMPUTER LOCKED              *
ECHO *=======================================*
```

```
CTTY COM1
UNLOCKER
:END

ECHO OFF
:   [*] TIMER.BAT [*]
:    == Stores current time ==
TIME<CR.ASC |FIND "Current" >TIME.$$$
COPY SET.ASC+RELEASE.ASC+TIME.$$$+RETURN.ASC TIMENOW.BAT
>NUL
TIMENOW

ECHO OFF
:   [*] UNLOCKER.BAT [*]
:    == Unlocks Computer at Time ==
:LOOP
IF EXIST ALARM.$$$ GOTO END
ECHO %NOW% >NOW.ASC
FIND "%UNLOCK%" NOW.ASC >READY.BAT
COMMAND /C READY
TIMER
GOTO LOOP
:END
CTTY CON
ECHO <alt-7>

ECHO OFF
:   [*] RELEASE.BAT [*]
ECHO NOW!>ALARM.$$$


:   [*] AUTOEXEC ADD [*]
:    == Alternate AUTOEXEC.BAT addition ==
TYPE DATE.ASC
INPUT
IF ERRORLEVEL 64 IF NOT ERRORLEVEL 65 GOTO RIGHT
LOCK 99:99
:RIGHT
```

---

[*] RELEASE.ASC [*]

```
COPY CON:RELEASE.ASC<Enter>
RELEASE<space><space>:<space><F6><Enter>
```

---

[*] SET.ASC [*]

```
COPY CON:SET.ASC<Enter>
SET NOW=<F6><Enter>
```

---

[*] RETURN.ASC [*]

HARD DISK SOLUTIONS WITH BATCH FILE UTILITIES

```
COPY CON:RETURN.ASC<Enter>
UNLOCKER<Enter>
<F6><Enter>
```

----

[*] DATE.ASC [*]

```
COPY CON:DATE.ASC<Enter>
Current date is October 31, 1980<Enter>
Enter new date (mm-dd-yy):<F6><Enter>
```

15
A Hard Disk Menu System

Complex computer systems like those equipped with hard disks have typically been hard to learn, or hard to use, but rarely both. Systems that are hard to learn include DOS, with its unforgiving command-line syntax. However, once you have mastered the intricacies of DOS, it is very easy to use, as you may type complex commands like:

```
FOR %%a IN (*.*) DO IF EXIST A:%%a COPY %%a B:
```

This book has probably been a great deal of help in resolving some of the mysteries of MS-DOS. Other systems are considered easy to learn, but difficult to use. Menus are an example of such a system. Because the user may select from a listing of choices, actual command syntax does not need to be learned. However, those who become familiar with the system find that wading through several levels of menus can become bothersome. Fortunately, MS-DOS provides the user with a choice: a menu-system shell can be set up for the neophyte or unsophisticated user, while the more advanced computer operator can work directly with DOS.

This chapter is designed to present a typical menu-system shell that might be used in businesses where operator turnover is frequent, where users spend time with the computer infrequently, or where an easy-to-learn menu system might be desirable for other reasons, such as to keep the user from messing with DOS or the hard disk!

The system consists of a group of batch files, each of which will be discussed separately. If you do not have the diskette accompanying this book, the files can be entered from the keyboard. Most are not really very long. However, note some of the conventions used to make the listings a bit more readable:

- Where Alt keys are to be used, they are so indicated: ⟨alt-255⟩, ⟨alt-186⟩, etc.
- Where a certain key is repeated, the number of repetitions are shown inside brackets:
  [27 ⟨alt-205⟩]
  You would enter ⟨alt-205⟩ 27 times.
- Keep in mind that INPUT.COM and all the batch files used by the menu must be in a subdirectory that can be found by DOS using its PATH.

Main Menu: MENU.BAT

This is the listing shown on the screen that allows users to choose from among five options:

```
1. Run Applications
2. Utilities
3. Back Up Hard Disk
4. Messages
5. DOS Command
```

The choice selected is determined by INPUT.COM and the ERRORLEVEL checking procedure used throughout this book. Each of the first four options calls up one of four appropriate batch files, APMEN.BAT, BACKMEN.BAT, UTILMEN.BAT, or MESSMEN.BAT.

The fifth option, DOS Command, actually sends the user into DOS, but changes the prompt to include a message, "TYPE MENU when finished," to remind the user to get back to the menu system when done.

Applications Menu: APMEN.BAT

This menu presents a choice of possible applications programs, including spreadsheet, word-processing, database manager, and telecommunications. The choices are rounded out with the DOS Command option again, as well as a new facility: a return to the main menu by typing X.

This batch file is presented as a skeleton for you to fill in with your own applications. Additional choices may be added to the menu as desired. The actual applications are started through a second batch file, AP.BAT. At each routine within APMEN.BAT, AP.BAT is summoned using a replaceable parameter that directs it to the proper application, for example:

```
AP LOTUS
AP WP PC-WRITE
```

This is done to provide you with the flexibility of specifying any parameters that your particular applications call for. When AP.BAT is accessed, the first parameter tells it which subdirectory to change to (assuming your applications reside in their own subdirectories, such as C:\LOTUS, C:\WP, etc.). The second parameter can be the program name or a parameter to be passed to the application.

Utility Menu: UTILMEN.BAT

This menu provides six choices:

```
1. Format a Disk
2. Go to BASIC
3. Purge a Disk
4. Norton Utilities
5. DOS Command
X  Exit to Main Menu
```

Formatting is carried out from within the batch file, allowing you to format a disk in drive A: only. The BASIC command loads BASICA, and then goes back to the utilities menu when the user exits BASICA by typing SYSTEM.

The purge choice illustrates how you can interface other utilities with a menu system. If the user has PURGE.BAT and PURGER.BAT on the hard disk, they can be accessed by typing the correct syntax shown.

Your favorite commercial utility can also be connected to the menu. Here, we've used the popular *Norton Utilities* as an example.

For communications, database management, and word processing, our example shows the "shareware" products PC-TALK, PC-WRITE, and PC-FILE. You would substitute the names of your own applications and include any special start-up commands required.

Hard Disk Backup: BACKMEN.BAT

Hard disk backup is streamlined through BACKMEN.BAT, which has built in the syntax for full disk backups and backing up only new files, as well as backup by specific date or directory. For the latter two, the user must actually type in the command but is shown how to do it. For restoring files, a separate RESTMEM.BAT file is accessed. It allows restoring all files, or prompted restoring.

A Simple Message System: MESSMEM.BAT

When two or more users access the same computer, they can leave messages for each other using this set of batch files. You may enter, retrieve, or kill messages. All messages are stored in a file using the recipient's last name. If the name is longer than eight characters, only the first eight characters should be used.

The actual messaging is done using three batch files called TO.BAT, READ.BAT, and SCRAP.BAT. The user may, for example, type:

```
TO BUSCH
```

The batch file will then open a file to copy from the console called TEMP.ASC. The user may then type the message (editing is not allowed, of course) and press F6 when finished. DOS will then add the message to a file consisting of the recipient's last name (eight-character limitation) plus the .MSG extension. Any future messages will be added to this, ad infinitum.

Typing:

```
READ BUSCH
```

will display file BUSCH.MSG through the MORE filter in (reasonably) convenient pages. After reading the file, the user will be provided the option of erasing it with:

```
SCRAP.BUSCH
```

This will allow the user to erase the file without reading it again.

That's about all there is to our menu system. Additional layers, HELP files, etc., can be added should you think they are needed. This system should provide a model for your own personalized menu.

```
ECHO OFF
: [*] MAIN MENU [*]
CLS
ECHO <alt-201>[27 <alt-205>]<alt-187>
ECHO <alt-186>       HARD DISK MENU         <alt-186>
ECHO <alt-200>[27 <alt-205>]<alt-188>
ECHO <alt-255>
ECHO <alt-201>[27 <alt-205>]<alt-187>
ECHO <alt-186>   1. Run Applications        <alt-186>
ECHO <alt-186>   2. Utilities               <alt-186>
ECHO <alt-186>   3. Back Up Hard Disk       <alt-186>
ECHO <alt-186>   4. Messages                <alt-186>
ECHO <alt-186>   5. DOS Command             <alt-186>
ECHO <alt-186>                              <alt-186>
ECHO <alt-186>       ENTER CHOICE:          <alt-186>
ECHO <atl-200>[27 <alt-205>]<alt-188>
:INPUT
INPUT
IF ERRORLEVEL 49 IF NOT ERRORLEVEL 50 GOTO APP
IF ERRORLEVEL 50 IF NOT ERRORLEVEL 51 GOTO UTIL
```

```
IF ERRORLEVEL 51 IF NOT ERRORLEVEL 52 GOTO BACKUP
IF ERRORLEVEL 52 IF NOT ERRORLEVEL 53 GOTO MESSAGES
IF ERRORLEVEL 53 IF NOT ERRORLEVEL 54 GOTO DOS
GOTO INPUT
:APP
APMEN
:UTIL
UTILMEN
:BACKUP
BACKMEN
:MESSAGES
MESSMEN
:DOS
CLS
ECHO Enter DOS command as usual.
PROMPT=TYPE MENU when finished.$_$n$g


ECHO OFF
: [*] APMEN.BAT [*]
:START
CLS
ECHO <alt-201>[27 <alt-205>]<alt-187>
ECHO <alt-186> * APPLICATIONS SUBMENU *     <alt-186>
ECHO <alt-200>[27 <alt-205>]<alt-188>
ECHO <alt-255>
ECHO <alt-201>[27 <alt-205>]<alt-187>
ECHO <alt-186>   1. Lotus 1-2-3            <alt-186
ECHO <alt-186>   2. Word Processing        <alt-186>
ECHO <alt-186>   3. Database Manager       <alt-186>
ECHO <alt-186>   4. Communications         <alt-186>
ECHO <alt-186>   5. DOS Command            <alt-186>
ECHO <alt-186>   X  Exit to Main Menu      <alt-186>
ECHO <alt-186>                             >alt-186>
ECHO <alt-186>      ENTER CHOICE:          <alt-186>
ECHO <alt-200>[27 <alt-205>]<alt-188>
:INPUT
INPUT
IF ERRORLEVEL 49 IF NOT ERRORLEVEL 50 GOTO LOTUS
IF ERRORLEVEL 50 IF NOT ERRORLEVEL 51 GOTO WP
IF ERRORLEVEL 51 IF NOT ERRORLEVEL 52 GOTO DB
IF ERRORLEVEL 52 IF NOT ERRORLEVEL 53 GOTO COMM
IF ERRORLEVEL 53 IF NOT ERRORLEVEL 54 GOTO DOS
IF ERRORLEVEL 120 IF NOT ERRORLEVEL 121 GOTO MAIN
IF ERRORLEVEL 88 IF NOT ERRORLEVEL 89 GOTO MAIN
GOTO INPUT
:MAIN
MENU
:LOTUS
AP LOTUS
:WP
```

```
AP WP PC-WRITE
:DB
AP DB PC-FILE
:COMM
AP COMM PC-TALK
:DOS
CLS
ECHO Enter DOS command as usual.
ECHO Type "MENU" when finished.
ECHO ON
PROMPT=TYPE MENU when finished.$_$n$g

ECHO OFF
: [*] AP.BAT [*]
C:
CD C:\%1
%2
APMEN

ECHO OFF
: [*] UTILMEN.BAT [*]
CLS
:START
ECHO <alt-201>[27 <alt-205>]<alt-187>
ECHO <alt-186>    * UTILITIES SUBMENU *    <alt-186>
ECHO <alt-200>[27 <alt-205>]<alt-188>
ECHO <alt-255>
ECHO <alt-201>[27 <alt-205>]<alt-187>
ECHO <alt-186>   1. Format a Disk          <alt-186>
ECHO <alt-186>   2. Go to BASIC            <alt-186>
ECHO <alt-186>   3. Purge a Disk           <alt-186>
ECHO <alt-186>   4. Norton Utilities       <alt-186>
ECHO <alt-186>   5. DOS Command            <alt-186>
ECHO <alt-186>   X  Exit to Main Menu      <alt-186>
ECHO <alt-186>                             <alt-186>
ECHO <alt-186>       ENTER CHOICE:         <alt-186>
ECHO <alt-200>[27 <alt-205>]<alt-188>
:INPUT
INPUT
IF ERRORLEVEL 49 IF NOT ERRORLEVEL 50 GOTO FORMAT
IF ERRORLEVEL 50 IF NOT ERRORLEVEL 51 GOTO BASIC
IF ERRORLEVEL 51 IF NOT ERRORLEVEL 52 GOTO PURGE
IF ERRORLEVEL 52 IF NOT ERRORLEVEL 53 GOTO NORTON
IF ERRORLEVEL 53 IF NOT ERRORLEVEL 54 GOTO DOS
IF ERRORLEVEL 120 IF NOT ERRORLEVEL 121 GOTO MAIN
IF ERRORLEVEL 88 IF NOT ERRORLEVEL 89 GOTO MAIN
GOTO INPUT
:MAIN
MENU
:FORMAT
ECHO Will format disk in drive A: only.
```

```
FORMAT A:
GOTO START
:BASIC
C:
BASICA
GOTO START
:PURGE
ECHO TYPE PURGE [filename]
GOTO END
:NORTON
C:
CD \NORTON
NU
UTILMEN
:COMM
AP COMM PC-TALK
:DOS
CLS
:END
ECHO Type "MENU" when finished.
ECHO ON
PROMPT=TYPE MENU when finished.$_$n$g


ECHO OFF
: [*] BACKMEN.BAT [*]
:START
CLS
ECHO <alt-201>[27 <alt-205>]<alt-187>
ECHO <alt-186>     * BACKUP SUBMENU *      <alt-186>
ECHO <alt-200>[27 <alt-205>]<alt-188>
ECHO <alt-255>
ECHO <alt-201>[27 <alt-205>]<alt-187>
ECHO <alt-186>   1. Full Disk Backup       <alt-186>
ECHO <alt-186>   2. Backup New Files       <alt-186>
ECHO <alt-186>   3. Backup by Date         <alt-186>
ECHO <alt-186>   4. Backup Directory       <alt-186>
ECHO <alt-186>   5. Restore                <alt-186>
ECHO <alt-186>   X  Exit to Main Menu      <alt-186>
ECHO <alt-186>                             <alt-186>
ECHO <alt-186>      ENTER CHOICE:          <alt-186>
ECHO <alt-200>[27 <alt-205>]<alt-188>
:INPUT
INPUT
IF ERRORLEVEL 49 IF NOT ERRORLEVEL 50 GOTO FULL
IF ERRORLEVEL 50 IF NOT ERRORLEVEL 51 GOTO NEW
IF ERRORLEVEL 51 IF NOT ERRORLEVEL 52 GOTO DATE
IF ERRORLEVEL 52 IF NOT ERRORLEVEL 53 GOTO DIRECTORY
IF ERRORLEVEL 53 IF NOT ERRORLEVEL 54 GOTO RESTORE
IF ERRORLEVEL 120 IF NOT ERRORLEVEL 121 GOTO MAIN
IF ERRORLEVEL 88 IF NOT ERRORLEVEL 89 GOTO MAIN
GOTO INPUT
```

```
:MAIN
MENU
:FULL
BACKUP C:\ A: /S
MENU
:NEW
BACKUP C:\ A: /S /M
MENU
:DATE
ECHO TYPE:
ECHO BACKUP C: A: /D:[date]
GOTO END
:DIRECTORY
ECHO TYPE:
ECHO BACKUP C: A:\[directory]
GOTO END
:RESTORE
RESTMEN
:END
ECHO Type "MENU" when finished.
ECHO ON
PROMPT=TYPE MENU when finished.$_$n$g


ECHO OFF
: [*] RESTMEN.BAT [*]
:START
CLS
ECHO <alt-201>[27 <alt-205>]<alt-187>
ECHO <alt-186>     * RESTORE SUBMENU *      <alt-186>
ECHO <alt-200>[27 <alt-205>]<alt-188>
ECHO <alt-255>
ECHO <alt-201>[27 <alt-205>]<alt-187>
ECHO <alt-186>   1. Restore all Files     <alt-186>
ECHO <alt-186>   2. Prompted Restore      <alt-186>
ECHO <alt-186>   X  Exit to Main Menu     <alt-186>
ECHO <alt-186>                            <alt-186>
ECHO <alt-186>      ENTER CHOICE:         <alt-186>
ECHO <alt-200>[27 <alt-205>]<alt-188>
:INPUT
INPUT
IF ERRORLEVEL 49 IF NOT ERRORLEVEL 50 GOTO ALL
IF ERRORLEVEL 50 IF NOT ERRORLEVEL 51 GOTO PROMPTED
IF ERRORLEVEL 120 IF NOT ERRORLEVEL 121 GOTO MAIN
IF ERRORLEVEL 88 IF NOT ERRORLEVEL 89 GOTO MAIN
GOTO INPUT
:MAIN
MENU
:ALL
RESTORE A: C:\ /S
MENU
:PROMPTED
```

```
RESTORE A: C:\ /S /P
MENU


ECHO OFF
: [*] MESSMEN.BAT [*]
:START
CLS
ECHO <alt-201>[27 <alt-205>]<alt-187>
ECHO <alt-186>      * MESSAGES SUBMENU *      <alt-186>
ECHO <alt-200>[27 <alt-205>]<alt-188>
ECHO <alt-255>
ECHO <alt-201>[27 <alt-205>]<alt-187>
ECHO <alt-186>   1. Enter Message            <alt-186>
ECHO <alt-186>   2. Retrieve Message         <alt-186>
ECHO <alt-186>   3. Kill Message             <alt-186>
ECHO <alt-186>   X  Exit to Main Menu        <alt-186>
ECHO <alt-186>                               <alt-186>
ECHO <alt-186>        ENTER CHOICE:          <alt-186>
ECHO <alt-200>[27 <alt-205>]<alt-188>
:INPUT
INPUT
IF ERRORLEVEL 49 IF NOT ERRORLEVEL 50 GOTO ENTER
IF ERRORLEVEL 50 IF NOT ERRORLEVEL 51 GOTO RETRIEVE
IF ERRORLEVEL 51 IF NOT ERRORLEVEL 52 GOTO KILL
IF ERRORLEVEL 120 IF NOT ERRORLEVEL 121 GOTO MAIN
IF ERRORLEVEL 88 IF NOT ERRORLEVEL 89 GOTO MAIN
GOTO INPUT
:MAIN
MENU
:ENTER
PROMPT=TYPE TO [lastname]$_$n$g
GOTO END
:RETRIEVE
PROMPT=TYPE READ [lastname]$_$n$g
GOTO END
:KILL
PROMPT=TYPE SCRAP [lastname]$_$n$g
:END


ECHO OFF
:  [*] TO.BAT [*]
IF "%1"=="" GOTO HELP
CLS
ECHO Enter message.  Press F6 [Enter] when done.
ECHO +----+----+----+----+----+----+----+----+----+----+
COPY CON:TEMP.$$$
TYPE TEMP.$$$>>%1.MSG
ERASE TEMP.$$$
GOTO END
:HELP
```

```
ECHO Type TO [lastname]
:END
MESSMEN

ECHO OFF
:   [*] READ.BAT [*]
IF "%1"=="" GOTO HELP
MORE<%1.MSG
ECHO <alt-255>
ECHO-----------------------------------
ECHO Kill all these messages?
INPUT
IF ERRORLEVEL 121 IF NOT ERRORLEVEL 122 GOTO KILL
IF ERRORLEVEL 89 IF NOT ERRORLEVEL 90 GOTO KILL
GOTO END
:KILL
ERASE %1.MSG
GOTO END
:HELP
ECHO Type TO [lastname]
:END
MESSMEN

ECHO OFF
:   [*] SCRAP.BAT [*]
IF "%1"=="" GOTO HELP
ERASE %1*.*
GOTO END
:HELP
ECHO Type SCRAP [lastname]
:END
MESSMEN
```

16
Hard Disk Backup Techniques

Frequent backups are a fact of life for hard disk users. After all, even the most reliable hard disk drive can fail, and with 20 to 30 megabytes of information stored on the typical drive, the stakes are very high for the businessperson.

A good rule of thumb is to back up your files on a timetable set by how much data you can afford to lose. If information is keyed into a database and then the original documents destroyed or discarded, there may be *no* margin for error. All hard disk data in such cases must be backed up immediately—preferably several times.

If a day's worth of work, or a week's, can be reconstructed conveniently, a daily or weekly backup schedule can be more practical. However, once a schedule is established, stick to it.

In part one we looked at the various media alternatives to a hard disk, including regular floppies, high-capacity floppies, tape drives, and optical disks. One of these is likely to be your medium for hard disk backup, since the ability to remove the data to a safe location is one of the key requirements of a good backup system.

Now, we'll look at the various ways of backing up data.

File-by-File Copying: Manual Methods

It is entirely possible to efficiently back up a hard disk onto floppy disks simply by making backup copies of each file you create. You can format a blank disk for each subdirectory on your hard disk, and copy files over to the diskette either en masse or a few files at a time as they are created. This method requires no software expertise and is particularly effective if a given user creates only a few files a day and can remember to back them up to floppy disks at the end of the day.

You can also create batch files that automate the chore somewhat. While this book was being written, the author copied all the files from the hard disk to two duplicate sets of two floppy disks at the end of the working day. All the chapters from 1 to 8 were named CH1.DOC through CH8.DOC. The rest were named CH-9 to CH-16. A simple batch file was created.

```
ECHO OFF
ECHO Insert Diskettes for Chapters 1-8 in A: and B:
PAUSE
COPY C:\WP\HARDDISK\CH?.DOC A: >NUL
COPY C:\WP\HARDDISK\CH?.DOC B: >NUL
ECHO Insert Diskettes for Chapters 9-16 in A: and B:
PAUSE
COPY C:\WP\HARDDISK\CH-*.DOC A: >NUL
COPY C:\WP\HARDDISK\CH-*.DOC B: >NUL
```

You can create your own custom batch files for such backup methods. It is easy to include IF EXIST lines in the batch file that will *only* back up files if they already exist on a given floppy, to update with the latest version, or only if they do *not,* to avoid overwriting files with the same name.

Backup Using XCOPY

DOS 3.2 introduced the XCOPY command. XCOPY supports 3½-inch diskettes, but also has some handy features suitable for backup. For example, the program is very fast. Unlike COPY, which reads and writes files individually, XCOPY will read into memory from the source disk as many files as will fit and then will write them to the destination disk. XCOPY also allows switches that affect how the utility operates. Briefly, these are:

- /S
  Example: **XCOPY C:\WP \LETTERS\ *.* A: /S**

Will copy files from nested subdirectories, creating any required new directories on the target diskette. This allows copying from diskette to diskette or from hard disk to diskette while keeping the same directory structure. Where DISKCOPY will copy an entire diskette to another, it produces a mirror image with all the file fragmentation of the original. XCOPY with the /S switch keeps the subdirectory structure, but copies the files as entities to produce unfragmented files on the destination. This also allows you to copy to a diskette that already has files on it without erasing them.

- /P
  Example: **XCOPY C:\WP\ *.* A: /P**
  Will prompt you about each file, asking if you want to copy it (similar to the utility provided with this book for users of DOS 3.1 or earlier).
- /D [date]
  Example: **XCOPY C:\ *.* A: /D:06-08-88**
  Will copy only files created or changed on that date or a later date.
- /M
  Example: **XCOPY C:\ *.* A: /M /S**
  Will copy only the files created or changed since the last backup, and will prompt you for a new disk when the old one is full. Each file has associated with it an "archive" bit which is set to 1 when it is created or changed, and set to 0 by backup programs like XCOPY. If XCOPY sees a file with a 1 archive bit, it will copy it (if it meets the other file specifications), and then set the archive bit to 0.

If you have DOS 3.2 or later, you can use XCOPY's capabilities in your own batch files to build powerful automated backup routines.

Backup with BACKUP

All the methods discussed so far copy your files to the backup media in the form of files that can be individually accessed and

HARD DISK SOLUTIONS WITH BATCH FILE UTILITIES

copied back to your hard disk or to any other storage device. DOS also provides a special routine, BACKUP and its complementary RESTORE command, which puts hard disk information onto floppy diskettes in a special format that gets the most use from the space available on the diskettes. The syntax for the BACKUP command is as follows:

```
BACKUP [d1:][path][filename] [d2:][/S][/M][/A][/D:mm-dd-yy]
```

- d1:—the source drive. With DOS 2.x, this drive specification must be C:, except in those cases where the user has more than one hard disk (D:, etc.). With DOS 3.x and later versions, the source diskette can be any drive, allowing the BACKUP command to be used to back up from one diskette to another.
- path—the path name of the directory to be backed up. If no path is specified, the currently logged directory is used by BACKUP.
- filename—you may use wildcards to represent more than one file. If *.* is used, or if this parameter is omitted, all the files in the directory indicated will be backed up.
- d2:—the destination drive. With DOS 2.x and systems with one floppy drive, this specification must be A:. With DOS 3.x and higher, any drive can be used.
- /S—as with XCOPY, the /S tells DOS to copy all the files in the subdirectories beneath the one indicated. So

```
BACKUP C:\ A: /S
```

would copy all the files on a hard disk to A:, with the user prompted to put in new diskettes as they fill.

- /M—as with XCOPY, the /M switch tells DOS only to copy those files that have not been backed up, that is, that have an attribute bit set to 1.
- A—tells DOS *not* to erase the files that may currently be on a diskette. New files will be added to those already on the diskette.

- /D:mm-dd-yy—like XCOPY, BACKUP can be used to copy only the files that have been created or changed after the date included with the /D switch.

To use BACKUP, make sure you have sufficient diskettes on hand. With 360K floppies, you will need 28 to 30 for a 10-megabyte hard disk and 56 to 60 for a 20-megabyte disk. When high-capacity diskettes are used, 8 or 9 will be needed for a 10-megabyte drive, and 17 or 18 for a 20-megabyte drive. BACKUP will supply numbers for the diskettes as they are used, which you can then apply to them using labels. Most users keep double sets of backup disks. That is, each new backup is made to the oldest set, so if a problem occurs, the more recent backup floppies are still available. Then, the newer set becomes the oldest to be used for the next backup.

Backed up files can be restored to the hard disk using the RESTORE command. The syntax for RESTORE is as follows:

```
RESTORE [d1:] [d2:][path][filename] [/S][/P]
```

- d1:—the source drive. This parameter is not optional.
- d2:—the destination drive. If not specified, C: will be used.
- path—the directory where the restored files are to be routed. If not specified, the currently logged directory on the destination drive is used.
- filename—you may use wildcards to specify restoring only certain file names. If this parameter is omitted, all the files in the specified directory are restored.
- /S—the reverse of the BACKUP command, causing all the subdirectories below the one specified to be restored as well.
- /P—a handy feature. It will prompt the user before overwriting files that have been changed since the last backup, or files that have been marked by ATTRIB as read-only. This prevents accidentally restoring a file that has been changed and hence is more up-to-date than the one that was backed up. You can also mark files with ATTRIB to protect them from being overwritten by RESTORE.

Using ATTRIB

ATTRIB was introduced with DOS 3.x. Its syntax is as follows:

```
ATTRIB [+R][-R] [d:][path][filename]
```

- +R—sets a file to read-only status.
- −R—sets a file to read/write, which allows it to be changed, erased, or overwritten.
- d:—the drive where the file resides.
- path—the path where the file resides.
- filename—the file's name.

Example: **ATTRIB +R C:\WP\LETTERS\DB *.***

This would protect all the files in subdirectory C:\WP\LETTERS that begin with DB from accidental erasure or overwriting.

Backing Up with Other Media

Many users rely on other media for faster, more unattended backup procedures. Removable hard disk cartridges can be used, although these have a reputation for susceptibility to damage from dirt and accidents like dropping. More common are removable tape cartridges, either of the streaming or non-streaming type.

Streaming tapes are simple, low-cost, reliable media that capture a hard disk's data in one fell swoop as the software directs the information out to the drive in a continuous data stream. Restoration occurs at a similar pace.

Nonstreaming drives start and stop under control of the computer, providing great flexibility in matching computer and backup medium speeds. However, such drives and media are more complex and higher in cost.

Appendix A: Scan Codes

The following is a table of scan codes for the IBM PC family and many compatibles. Note that some compatible computers, like the Tandy line, may have different scan codes for some keys, because of a nonstandard layout.

When using INPUT.COM, only the second code of an extended scan code will be returned, so that Alt-N will indicate the same 49 value as the number 1. Possible conflicts in your own batch file programming should be rare, however.

SCAN CODES FOR IBM PC

Key	Code	Shift	Control	Alt
A	97	65	1	0;30
B	98	66	2	0:48
C	99	67	3	0;46
D	100	68	4	0;32
E	101	69	5	0;18
F	102	70	6	0;33
G	103	71	7	0;34
H	104	72	8	0;35
I	105	73	9	0;23
J	106	74	10	0;36
K	107	75	11	0;37
L	108	76	12	0;38
M	109	77	13	0;50
N	110	78	14	0;49

HARD DISK SOLUTIONS WITH BATCH FILE UTILITIES

Key	Code	Shift	Control	Alt
O	111	79	15	0;24
P	112	80	16	0;25
Q	113	81	17	0;16
R	114	82	18	0;19
S	115	83	19	0;31
T	116	84	20	0;20
U	117	85	21	0;22
V	118	86	22	0;47
W	119	87	23	0;17
X	120	88	24	0;45
Y	121	89	25	0;21
Z	122	90	26	0;44
1	49	33		0;120
2	50	64		0;121
3	51	35		0;122
4	52	36		0;123
5	53	37		0;124
6	54	94		0;125
7	55	38		0;126
8	56	42		0;127
9	57	40		0;128
0	48	41		0;129
-	45	95		0;130
=	61	43		0;131
TAB	9	0;15		
SPACE	57			

Extended Scan Codes for Numeric Keypad and Function Keys

Key	Code	Shift	Control	Alt
F1	0;59	0;84	0;94	0;104
F2	0;60	0;85	0;95	0;105
F3	0;61	0;86	0;96	0;106
F4	0;62	0;87	0;97	0;107
F5	0;63	0;88	0;98	0;108
F6	0;64	0;89	0;99	0;109
F7	0;65	0;90	0;100	0;110
F8	0;66	0;91	0;101	0;111
F9	0;67	0;92	0;102	0;112

Key	Code	Shift	Control	Alt
F10	0;68	0;93	0;103	0;113
F11	0;69			
F12	0;70			
Home	0;71	55	0;119	
Crs-Up	0;72	56		
Pg Up	0;73	57	0;132	
Crs-Lf	0;75	52	0;115	
Crs-Rt	0;77	54	0;116	
End	0;79	49	0;117	
Crs-Dn	0;80	50		
Pg Dn	0;81	51	0;118	
Ins	0;82	48		
Del	0;83	46		
PrtSc			0;114	

Appendix B: Glossary

AUTOEXEC.BAT: An ASCII file placed in the root directory of the disk. It contains a list of commands that will be carried out by DOS automatically during the boot-up operation. This file allows the user to load memory-resident programs, specify a PATH to be used by DOS to search for system files, and perform other tasks that configure the system.

Bernoulli drive: A mass-storage device using flexible magnetic media and relying on the Bernoulli effect to keep the disk and read/write heads separated by a thin cushion of air. These drives offer the same storage capacity as smaller hard disk drives, have access times that are somewhat slower, but have the advantage of providing removable media and freedom from data-damaging head crashes.

BIOS: The Basic Input/Output System of a computer, consisting of a piece of computer code, provided on read-only memory (ROM) chips and used to govern basic system-level functions.

Bootstrap: A very short set of computer instructions, usually designed to do nothing but load into the computer a longer program that carries out the actual loading of the operating system. On hard disks, the boot sector is found on the first sector of the first track of the first surface to be read by the system.

CD-ROM: Compact disk read-only memory. An optical disk mass-storage device that, like all optical disks, uses pits written on the disk by laser to convey information. CD-ROMS are encoded with information during manufacture and cannot be written to by the user. They provide a means of distributing large databases on one compact medium.

Cluster: The smallest unit of disk space that can be allocated by DOS. For hard disks, a cluster may be 4 sectors (512 bytes each), which is 2,048 bytes, or 16 sectors for a total of 8,192 bytes. Cluster size has a bearing on how efficiently DOS operates. Smaller clusters waste less space on the disk, but larger clusters allow DOS to collect more information at one time.

CONFIG.SYS: Another ASCII file, interpreted by DOS on booting, if present in the root directory of the boot disk. CONFIG.SYS is acted on *before* AUTOEXEC.BAT, but may not contain anything other than specific commands that specify device drivers to be used, or that set other system configuration factors such as the number of buffers to be allocated, size of the environment, etc.

Contiguous: In reference to hard disks, contiguous sectors are those that are arranged consecutively on the disk. DOS tries to allocate sectors to a file contiguously, so that the disk drive can read as many sectors of a file as it can with a mimimum amount of read/write head movement. However, as a hard disk fills, the unallocated sectors gradually become spread out and fragmented, forcing DOS to choose more and more noncontiguous sectors. Fragmented files can be much slower to access.

Coprocessor: An additional microprocessor used in tandem with the main processor. IBM PCs and compatibles typically have sockets for an 8087, 80287, or 80387 math coprocessor designed to offload number crunching tasks from the main microprocessor, producing much faster operation for applications involving much computation, such as spreadsheet recalculation.

Cylinder: The "stack" of tracks on all the platters of a hard disk drive, all the same distance from the center of the disk, which can be read simultaneously by the read/write heads.

Device driver: A software module that tells DOS how to control a given piece of hardware, such as a printer, monitor, disk drive, or keyboard. ANSI.SYS and VDISK.SYS are device drivers supplied with DOS. Others are supplied by manufacturers of peripherals.

DOS: Disk operating system. The control program of the computer which oversees how the system interfaces with the user and peripherals, including disks.

Dynamic RAM: A type of memory that must be electrically refreshed many times each second, or else the contents will be lost. PCs and compatibles use dynamic RAM to store programs, data, and the operating system.

Environment: An area of memory set aside to keep track of information, such as the system prompt. The user can also define variables to be placed in this environment through the SET command.

ESDI: Enhanced small device interface. A spin-off of the ST412 interface, this link between disk drives and PCs has a faster, 10-megabit per second, transfer rate and supports additional data-encoding methods. Device Systems Interface.

FAT: File allocation table. A special area on the disk that tracks how each cluster is assigned to various files.

File: A collection of information, usually data or a program, that has been given a name and allocated sectors by the FAT.

File-oriented backup: Any backup system that stores information in files, just as they are stored on the disk. Such systems allow easier access or restoration of a particular file.

Flux changes: Reversals in the magnetic orientation of the magnetic material on a disk, used to indicate the presence of a binary 1.

FM: Frequency modulation. A disk-encoding scheme in which each data bit is followed by a clock bit.

Hierarchical: In hard disk terminology, the structuring of directories such that each subdirectory has one parent, but may have several child directories, branching out in a treelike structure.

High-level format: The formatting performed by FORMAT.COM, in which information needed by DOS to use the disk is written.

Image-oriented backup: Any backup system that creates a mirror image of the disk, without regard to the files themselves. With such systems, the entire disk has to be restored from the backup medium to allow access to the files.

Induce: To cause an electrical field to be generated. As the read head of a disk drive passes over the media, the flux changes that have been written to the disk induce an electrical signal that can be interpreted by the drive controller to reconstruct the original information written to the disk.

Instructions: The basic capabilities of a microprocessor, allowing the chip to load information in registers, move it to other registers, increment the data, add or subtract data from registers, and so forth.

Intelligent: Having sufficient programming built-in to carry out certain tasks independently. An intelligent disk drive can accept requests from DOS, locate the data, and deliver it without detailed instructions on how to do the physical I/O.

Interactive: Allowing user input during run-time.

Interleave: The alternating of logical disk sectors to allow the hard disk time to process the information from one sector before the next is presented. Without interleave, a slow controller would allow reading only one sector per revolution.

Label: On a hard disk, the volume name applied immediately after high-level formatting, if the /V switch was specified, or by use of the LABEL command. In batch files, a label is a line prefixed with a colon, and is used to direct control from other parts of the batch file using the GOTO subcommand.

Landing zone: A location on the disk where no data is stored and, therefore, the read/write head may safely come to rest on the disk surface. Some drives automatically retract the heads to this landing zone when the computer is turned off. Others require a special program to be run, as when the computer will be shipped or moved.

Latency: The time needed for the hard disk to finish rotating to the first sector of a track so the read/write head can begin writing information or reading the track. The *average* latency time is usually included in the access time of a given hard disk. For an ST506 drive rotating at 3,600 RPM, the maximum latency would be one full revolution, or 16.67 milliseconds. Average latency would be half that, or 8.3 milliseconds.

Logical: Any feature not physically present, but defined anyway for convenience. The physical sectors on a hard disk are arranged contiguously. Logically, they may be arranged in alternating fashion through interleaving.

Low-level formatting: The most basic formatting done on the hard disk to prepare it for partitioning and high-level formatting. During this procedure, which is often done by the manufacturer, any bad sectors are locked out.

Macro: A series of commands that can be triggered at the press of a key or two. Many applications programs, as well as utilities like *SuperKey* and *ProKey*, allow the users to develop their own macros for frequently used command sequences.

MFM: Modified frequency modulation. Another disk-encoding method.

Oersted: A measure of the coercivity of a magnetic medium, or its ability to capture and retain information. Usually abbreviated Oe.

Overlays: Portions of a program that are called into memory as needed, overlaying the previous redundant section of the program. Using overlays allows programs to run that are too big to fit into memory all at once.

Parameter: A qualifier that defines more precisely what a program such as DOS is to do.

Partition: A part of a disk set aside for use by a particular operating system. One partition on a hard disk is bootable. The others, if any, may become the active partition through use of the FDISK program.

Path: A listing of directory names in an order that defines the location of a particular file.

Physical: A feature that exists in reality.

Pixel: A picture element of a screen image: one "dot" of the collection that make up an image.

Redirection: Rerouting input or output to or from the device for which it was originally headed. For example, you may send screen output to the printer using a command like DIR>PRN, or send it to a file: DIR>MYFILE.ASC.

Registers: The basic special-purpose memory locations of a microprocessor, used to carry out its instructions during the computing process.

RISC: Reduced instruction set computer. A computer system that has a special microprocessor with fewer instructions, and which therefore operates faster. Such systems depend on the software for functions that formerly were handled by the microprocessor.

RLL: Run Length Limited. An encoding system for hard disks that is 50 percent more efficient in the density of information that can be recorded. Therefore, hard disks using RLL have 50 percent more capacity and a data transfer rate that is 50 percent faster.

SCSI: Small computer systems interface, also called SASI, for Shugart Associates System Interface. An intelligent interface that can be used for a broad range of devices, including hard disks, tape drives, optical disks, and scanners.

Serial: Passing information 1 bit at a time in sequential order.

Static RAM: Memory that does not need to be refreshed, and which therefore does not lose its contents when power to the computer is turned off.

ST506: The most popular hard disk interface, originally defined by Seagate Technology for its 5-megabyte 5¼-inch hard disk drive. It uses two sets of drive signals. One carries the control and status information for up to four hard disk drives. The control signal selects and manages the drive and head used for read or write tasks. The status signal reports error conditions and indicates when the drive is ready.

The second set of signals contain the data itself. Given the most common encoding schemes, the ST506 interface has a transfer rate of 5 megabits per second.

ST412: An enhancement to ST506, this interface is used in the IBM PC-AT and other computers. The chief difference is that ST412 controllers aren't limited by the stepping rate of the drive: step pulses can be issued and stored in a buffer until the head is ready to move again. As a result, the ST412 controller is not tied up waiting for the drive and can process information.

Subdirectory: A directory created within another directory and storing its own separate files.

Substrate: A base material that is coated with another. For example, flexible polyester forms the substrate onto which a floppy disk's magnetic coating is placed. For hard disks, the substrate is most frequently a rigid aluminum platter.

System-level interface: An interface over which information is passed in logical form, directly from the device to the computer system, without the need for dedicated signal lines.

Transfer rate: The speed at which information can be read from a disk. With hard disks, this is typically 5 megabits per second, although new, denser encoding schemes and more advanced interfaces have increased this speed.

Tree-structured directories: The hierarchical structure of a DOS directory using parent and child directories.

Unfragmented: A hard disk that has most of its files stored in consecutive sectors, and not spread out over the disk. Such an arrangement allows more efficient reading of data with less time required to move the read/write head to gather the information.

Virtual disk: An electronic, or "RAM", disk created in memory to mimic a real disk drive—only much faster. DOS 3.x and later versions were supplied with VDISK.SYS, a device driver that allows creating multiple virtual disks in memory.

Volume: The largest hard disk entity that DOS is able to deal with. For example, a single physical disk can be divided into two or more logical disks created as separate volumes. DOS may see one volume as drive C: and the other as drive D: even though both exist on the same physical drive.

WORM: Write once read many (or mostly). Optical disk technology that allows writing to the disk by the user, although a given section cannot be erased and reused.

Appendix C: Quick Guide to Using the Utilities

If You Have the Accompanying Diskette

Create a subdirectory called C:\BATCHES and copy all the files in the root directory of the diskette over to that subdirectory. If you plan to use the hard disk security feature, copy the files in the subdirectory LOCKER over to a new subdirectory on your hard disk called C:\LOCKER.

If You Will Be Typing in the Files

The utilities are generally batch files. These are explained in chapters 10 and 11. Batch files are simple ASCII files that can be typed in from the keyboard by typing COPY CON:filename. Press F6 when you are done. You may not edit files this way, however. Some special characters are indicated as ⟨alt-xxx⟩. Hold down the Alt key while typing in the numbers indicated. Use the numeric keypad, and not the row of numbers at the top of your screen. Release the Alt key, and the character you have typed will appear on the screen, sometimes represented by a set of symbols. For example, Alt-7 will appear as ^G, or Control-g, its equivalent.

Batch files can also be entered from any word processor that can write ASCII files. This is sometimes called nondocument mode. Some word-processing programs will accept Alt key combinations. With others, you must experiment to see how to produce the characters. For example, with *DisplayWrite*, you can reproduce some of the characters indicated in this book as follows:

    Alt-Q = Alt-201
    Alt-Z = Alt-200
    Alt-C = Alt-188
    Alt-V = Alt-186
    Alt-E = Alt-187
    Alt-R = Alt-205

Check your own word-processor manual to see how to write ASCII files and enter special characters.

Other Considerations

You should add a line in your PATH statement telling DOS how to find these files. This should be placed in your AUTOEXEC.BAT file:

```
PATH C:\BATCHES;C:\LOCKER;C:\ . . . etc.
```

If you don't understand PATH or AUTOEXEC.BAT files and still want to get started immediately, read chapter 8 for a rundown on what you need to know.

Some of the utilities, particularly the LOCK series, require some changes to your CONFIG.SYS file as well. Most commonly, you will need to add DEVICE = ANSI.SYS to accommodate those utilities using key redefinition. The LOCK utilities make heavy use of the environment, so you will need a line like this in CONFIG.SYS:

```
SHELL=COMMAND.COM /P /E:60 (For DOS 3.1)
SHELL=COMMAND.COM /P /E:960 (For DOS 3.2 or later)
```

The LOCK utilities can also be more effective if used with a RAM disk. VDISK.SYS is one such device driver; there are

APPENDIX C: QUICK GUIDE TO USING THE UTILITIES

others supplied by manufacturers of multifunction boards, as well as by software vendors and public-domain sources. For VDISK, insert this line in CONFIG.SYS:

```
DEVICE=VDISK.SYS 15
```

Again, if you don't know what CONFIG.SYS is, read chapter 9 for an explanation.

Appendix D: Hard Disk Troubleshooting

Hard disk drives are frequently rated in terms of *mean time between failures,* or MTBF, which is a way of measuring the average reliability of the overall subsystem. That is, if your organization has 100 hard disk drives rated at 10,000 hours MTBF, half of them will fail *before* 10,000 hours and half of them will fail *after* 10,000 hours. A given disk drive may fail in the first hour or two of use, or can operate trouble-free for 20,000 hours or more.

Keep in mind that even at 10,000 hours MTBF, half of the disk drives can be operated 8 hours a day, 250 days a year, for 5 years before failure. However, after many trouble-free hours, you may still find yourself with an inoperable computer. This Appendix provides some tips for troubleshooting some common problems. This is *not* an installation guide; it is assumed that your hard disk has been operating properly for some period of time.

Symptom: Disk seems to access files much slower than previously, although it otherwise works normally.

Problem: Your hard disk has become *fragmented.* While DOS attempts to store files contiguously when possible, as files are continually stored and deleted on the hard disk, many small areas are left on the disk and used to store later files. As a result, the hard disk read/write heads must move over broad

HARD DISK SOLUTIONS WITH BATCH FILE UTILITIES

expanses of the platters to locate all the sectors belonging to a file. As the disk becomes full, this process can take much longer than before.

Solution: There are utility programs on the market that optimize file arrangement on the hard disk. These copy as many files as possible to contiguous areas of the disk, erase old groups of files, and thus free up additional areas of the disk for contiguous storage. The process repeats as long as necessary to optimize storage. Such utilities work best if your hard disk is not too full to begin with.

However, no special program is needed. Simply back up your entire hard disk, copying by *file* using COPY or XCOPY. It would be a good idea to perform this backup twice. Then erase all the files on the hard disk and remove the subdirectories. If you wish, you can do this with FORMAT. Then, recreate your directory structure and copy the files back. They will be placed contiguously on the disk. This is a slow procedure, but generally needs to be done once a year. It can usually be done in conjunction with an annual archiving of last year's files, or some other housekeeping chore.

Symptom: Your hard disk has *always* seemed slower than similar disks used by others in your organization.

Problem: The other hard disks may be set for a faster interleave ratio than yours, perhaps 2:1 versus your 1:1. This allows the disk to access more sectors per revolution, if the controller and computer can handle the higher speed.

Solution: Perform a backup as described earlier, and then use the low-level formatting program to reformat the disk at a different interleave ratio. The instructions provided with the utilities disk will explain exactly how to do this.

Symptom: Hard disk does not boot.

Problem: With IBM PCs and PC-XTs and some other models, listen at the left side of the computer, by the air vents, as the power is switched on. A split second after the power switch is thrown, a tiny click will usually be heard from the internal

APPENDIX D: HARD DISK TROUBLESHOOTING

speaker as power is applied to the motherboard. If no click is heard, one possible cause of the problem is a faulty power supply *even though the power supply fan continues to operate.*

Solution: Replace power supply. This costs less than $100, and in most model PCs and compatibles is one of the easiest components for the user to replace. Don't attempt to repair the power supply yourself unless you are qualified.

Symptom: Hard disk does not boot.

Problem: If the computer otherwise functions normally (that is, it goes through the power-on self test, and the monitor seems to be working), listen for the sound of the hard disk rotating. If no sound is heard, the hard disk itself or the power leading to it may be the cause.

Solution: Check controller card and/or connecting cables to hard disk, or the hard disk card itself, to see that all are properly seated. Sometimes simply removing the cards and/or cables and reinserting them can solve the problem. Don't attempt to take a hard disk apart and look for a problem yourself.

Symptom: Hard disk does not boot.

Problem: If the hard disk is rotating properly, but still will not boot (DOS attempts to load off drive A:, then goes to the hard disk without result), crucial sectors of the hard disk may have become damaged.

Solution: Boot from a floppy disk containing DOS. Attempt to get a directory of the hard disk. If you are successful, try copying the system over to the hard disk again, using SYS.

If you cannot get a directory of the drive, and valuable data has not been backed up, seek professional help from your organization's MIS director or from a computer store. Utility programs may be able to salvage information. You may also be able to back up (by file) information on the hard disk. The disk can often be put back into operation simply by low-level or

213

high-level formatting, and then reinstalling DOS and software as if it were a new disk.

The sector loss may have been caused by some DOS or operator error, or by a hardware problem such as a head crash. If the latter took place, the hard disk may be irreparably damaged. However, try these suggestions first before running to a service shop in a panic.

Symptom: Hard disk does not boot. It worked fine before a new expansion card was added.

Problem: You may have accidently moved a system board switch. Or the new card may conflict with your hard disk controller.

Solution: Double-check your system board switches. Most add-on cards will not conflict with a hard disk controller, except those that have a hard disk controller option. That is, some controller cards can operate floppy disks *and* hard disks, and some users install second hard disk controllers for an additional hard disk, not realizing that only one card may be needed. This most often occurs when a user attempts to install a hard disk card in a computer that has a bay-mounted hard disk and separate controller card. The bay-mount disk may be operable from the hard disk card's controller. It is likely that the two controllers can't be used in the same system, however.

Symptom: Hard disk doesn't work after system has been moved.

Problem: The read/write heads bounced up and down on the platter surface during the move and have damaged data areas, possibly including boot sectors and/or FAT or directory sectors.

Solution: Prior to moving the computer, park the drive heads using IBM diagnostics or a utility program provided with your hard disk. Note that you should *only* use the method recommended for your hard disk. Diagnostics or a generic head park utility may not work with a particular brand of hard disk. Also, some hard disks automatically retract the heads to a safe

APPENDIX D: HARD DISK TROUBLESHOOTING

landing zone when power is turned off, and so do not require a head-parking utility

With diagnostics, option 3 is labeled, PREPARE FIXED DISK FOR RELOCATION, or with the PC-AT, PREPARE SYSTEM FOR MOVING. Other utilities have similar messages. Immediately turn the computer off. If you type in any other command, the heads will be moved from the parked position.

Index

A

Access time, 19
ANSI .SYS, keyboard driver routine, 95-96, 125-129
Applications menu, ApMEN.BAT, 179
ASCII files
　finding strings, 144-145
　sorting, 147
ATTRIB
　backup, 194
　with other media, 194
AUTOEXEC.BAT, 92, 97-103
　and customizing task, 98
　and DOS, 98
　example file, 99-102
　and utilities, 98-99
Average latency, 19

B

BACKEN.BAT, backup, 180
Backup, 189-194
　ATTRIB, 194
　BACKEN.BAT, 180
　with BACKUP, 191-193
　　diskette used, 193
　　syntax for, 192
　file-by-file copying, 189-190
　RESTORE command, 193
　with XCOPY, 190-191
BASIC, 81
Batch files, 92
　AUTOEXEC.BAT, 97-103
　COMMAND.COM, calling second copy, 116-117
　environment variables, use of, 114-115
　explanation of, 97-98
　flexibility of, 106-107
　INPUT.COM, 111-112
　　and interactive batch files, 112
　menu system
　　applications menu, ApMEN.BAT, 179
　　backup, BACKMEN.BAT, 180
　　main menu, MENU.BAT, 178-179
　　message system, MESSMEN.BAT, 180-187
　　utility menu, UTILMEN.BAT, 179-180
　redefining keys with, 125-128
　redefining system prompt, 129-130
　replaceable parameters
　　calling labels, 120

217

INDEX

Batch files, (*continued*)
    quotes/equal sign, 119
    use of, 117–121
  restrictions with DOS, 98
  sample file, 105
  and start up of programs, 106
  sub commands, 107–114
    ECHO, 107–109
    FOR...IN...DO, 114
    GOTO, 109
    IF, 109–110
    REM, 109
    SHIFT, 119
Batch file utilities, 132–152
  ASCII files
    finding strings, 144–145
    sorting, 147
  comparing contents of disks/
    directories, 141–143
  duplicate files, deleting, 151–152
  entering information, 207–208
  file copying, prompted, 140–141
  FORMAT, 139–140
  locating files, 161–163
  menu utility (sample), 135
  moving files (one directory to another), 145–146
  paths, creating new, 147–149
  purging files interactively, 132–13
  REVERSE.BAT, 137–138
  subdirectories
    creating new, 149
    removing, 149–151
  updating hard disk's DOS, 143–144
Bay mounted hard disks, 49–51
  advantages of, 51
  capacities available, 51
  full height drives, 50
  half-height drives, 50
  installation of, 74–76
  versus hard disk cards, 51
Bernoulli-effect drives, 47–48
BIOS, and hard disk system, 25
Booting, failure to boot, 212–214

BREAK=ON or OFF, CONFIG.SYS file, 95
Bubble memory, 48
BUFFERS, CONFIG.SYS file, 94–95

C

CHDIR (CD) command, 86, 87
CHKDSK, 123
COMMAND.COM, calling second copy, 116–117
Command processor, SHELL, 96
Compatibles, expansion capacity, 59–60
Computers
  microprocessor, 5–6
  monitors, 6–7
  printers, 7
  storage, types of, 8–14
  See also Microcomputers.
CONFIG.SYS file, 41, 94–97
  commands
    BREAK=ON or OFF, 9
    BUFFERS, 94–95
    COUNTRY, 97
    DEVICE-driver, 9–96
    FILES, 95
    SHELL, 96
Controllers needed, 23, 24
Copying
  BACKUP, 191–193
    diskette used, 193
    syntax for, 192
  batch file utilities, 140–141
  file-by-file, 189–190
  from one disk to another, 50
  subdirectories, 90
  X COPY, 50
COUNTRY, CONFIG.SYS file, 97
Cursor movement sequences, listing of, 129–130
Cylinder size, 17–18

D

Database, on CD-ROM, 43–44
Data transfer rate, 18–19

INDEX

Device driver, 95-96
    CONFIG.SYS file, 95-96
Disks/directories, comparing
    contents of, 141-143
DOS, 81-92
    AUTOEXEC.BAT, 97-103
    and batch files, 94, 123-124
    CONFIG.SYS file, 94-97
    ERROR LEVEL, 110-111, 113
    extensions, groups of files, 83
    file allocation table (FAT), 55-56
    file naming, 89-90
        parts of name, 89
    filters
        FIND, 124
        MORE, 125
        SORT, 123-124
    formatting hard disk, 78-80
    and hard disk system, 25, 26-27
    hierarchical directory structure,
        83-86
    keyboard driver routine, ANSI
        .SYS, 95-96, 125-129
    paths
        batch files, 92
        setting up, 90-92
    root directory, 84-85
        TREE Command, 88
    subdirectories, 84-86
        CHDIR (CD) command, 86, 87
        copying of, 90
        creation of, 87
        moving through directories,
            86-87
        removal of, 87, 90
        RMR (RD) command, 87
        viewing contents of, 85-86, 89
    system environment, 90-91
        prompt, redefining, 91
    updating, 143-144
    versions of, 82
Duplicate files, deleting, 151-152

E

ECHO, subcommand, batch files,
    107-109

Enhanced small device interface
    (ESDI), 21
Encoding methods, 22-24
    controllers needed, 23, 24
    frequency modulation (FM), 23
    modified frequency modulation
        (MFM), 23
    RLL encoding systems, 23-24
Environment variables, batch
    files, use of, 114-11
Extensions, groups of files, 83
External hard disks, 54-55
    advantages/disadvantages of, 4-
        55

F

FAT (file allocation table), 55-56
    cluster size, 56
FDISK, 78-80
File cabinets, designing, file
    management, 156-158
File management, 153-163
    file name conventions,
        establishing, 158-160
    locating files, 161-163
    model, creating flow chart, 154-
        155
    subdirectory, file cabinets,
        designing, 156-158
File naming, 89-90
    conventions, establishing, for
        file management, 158-160
    parts of name, 89
FILES, CONFIG.SYS file, 95
Filters
    FIND, 124
    MORE, 125
    SORT, 123-124
FIND, 124
Floppy disks
    accessing information, 13
    rotation of, 13-14
FOR...IN...DO, subcommands,
    batch files, 114
FORMAT, batch file utilities, 139-
    140

219

INDEX

Formatting, 78-80
   and DOS partitions, 78-79
   FDISK, 78-80
   high level formatting, 78-79
   IS option and IV option, 79
   low-level format, 78, 79
Frequency modulation (FM), 23

G

GOTO, subcommand, batch files, 109

H

Half-height drives, 50
Hard disk cards, 52-54
   advantages, 52-53
   capacity available, 53
   increasing capacity, 53-54
   installation of, 52-53, 76-77
   ruggedizing, 51
   versus conventional hard disk, 51, 52
Hard disks
   alternatives to, 3-48
      Bernoulli-effect drives, 47-48
      bubble memory, 48
      high-capacity diskettes, 41-42
      optical disks, 43-46
      RAM, 36-41
      removable hard disks, 46
      tape cartridge storage, 46-47
   backup, 189-194
   benefits in use of, 29-33
   and BIOS, 25
   common objections to, 35-36
   and compatibles, 59-60
   and DOS, 25, 26-27
      file allocation table (FAT), 55-56
      formatting, 26
      partitioning, 26
   encoding methods, 22-24
      controllers needed, 23, 24
      frequency modulation (FM), 23
      modified frequency modulation (MFM), 23
      RLL encoding systems, 23-24
   file management, 153-163
   formatting, 78-80
      and DOS partitions, 78-79
      FDISK, 78-80
      high level formatting, 78-79
      IS option and IV option, 79
      low-level format, 78, 79
   head crash, 16
   and IBM PC, 57
   and IBM PC-AT, 60-61
   and IBM PC-XT, 58
   information-recording method, 15-16
   interfaces
      enhanced small device interface (ESDI), 21
      small computer system interface (SCSI), 22
      ST506/412 interface, 21
      system-level interfaces, 21-22
   menu system, 177-187
   physical features of, 17
   problems/troubleshooting, 211-215
      failure to boot, 212-214
      moving system, 214-215
      slow accessing, 211-212
   security, 165-176
   speed (affecting factors), 17-20
      access time, 19
      average latency, 19
      cylinder size, 17-18
      data transfer rate, 18-19
   types of
      bay mounted hard disks, 49-51
      external hard disks, 54-55
      hard disk cards, 52-54
Hardware compatibility, 59-60
Hierarchical directory structure, DOS, 83-86
High-capacity diskettes, 41-42
   advantages of, 42

INDEX

and hard disk problems, 42
Kodac media, 42
oersteds and, 41
High level formatting, 78-79
Hot key, 32

I

IBM PC, expansion capacity, 57
IBM PC-AT, expansion capacity, 60-61
IBM PC-XT, expansion capacity, 58
IF, subcommand, batch files, 109-110
INPUT.COM, 111-112
  and interactive batch files, 112
Integrated software, 31
Interfaces
  enhanced small device interface (ESDI), 21
  small computer system interface (SCSI), 22
  ST506/412 interface, 21
  system-level interfaces, 21-22

K

Keyboard driver routine
  ANSI.SYS, 95-96, 125-129
    Alt key combinations, 127
    function keys, 128
    scan codes, 127
Keyboard layout, COUNTRY, 97

L

Labels, and replaceable parameters, 120
Locating fields, 161-163
Low-level format, 78, 79

M

Main menu, MENU.BAT, 178-179
Menu system
  applications menu, ApMEN.BAT, 179
  backup, BACKMEN.BAT, 180
  main menu, MENU.BAT, 178-179
  menu utility (sample), batch file utilities, 135
  message system, MESSMEN.BAT, 180-187
  utility menu, UTILMEN.BAT, 179-180
Message system, MESSMEN.BAT, 180-187
Metastrings, listing of, 126
Microcomputers
  mass storage options, 63-67
    capacity and needs, 64-65, 66-67
    networked PCs, 66
    for stand-alone, 64-65, 66-67
    for word-processing, 66-67
Modified frequency modulation (MFM), 23
MORE, 125
Moving files (one directory to another), 14-146
Moving system, parking hard disk, 214-215
Moving through directories, 86-87

O

Operating systems
  and 80386 microprocessor, 81
  DOS, 81-92
  XENIX, 65, 78
Optical disks, 43-46
  compact disk read-only memory (CD-ROMs), 43-44
  erasable optical disks, 45
  write-once, read mostly (WORM) disk, 44

P

Parking hard disk, 214-215
Paths
  batch files, 92

221

INDEX

Paths, (*continued*)
   creating new, 147–149
   setting up, 90–92
Power-on self-test (POST), 77
Problems/troubleshooting, 211–215
   failure to boot, 212–214
   moving system, 214–215
   slow accessing, 211–212
Prompt (redefining), 91, 129–130
   cursor movement sequences, 129–130
   PROMPT command, metastrings, 126, 128
   two-line prompt, 129
Purging files interactively, batch file utilities, 132–135

R

RAM, 31, 36–41
   creating RAM disk, 102–103
   drawback of, 39
   explanation of, 36
   historical view, 37–38
   loss of, 40
   and virtual disks, 40
REM, subcommand, batch files, 109
Removable hard disks, 46
Removal of subdirectories, 87, 90
Replaceable parameters
   calling labels, 120
   quotes/equal sign, 119
   use of, 117–121
REVERSE.BAT, batch file utilities, 137–138
RLL encoding systems, 23–24
RMDIR (RD) command, 87
ROM chip, 25
Root directory, 84–8
   TREE Command, 88

S

Scan codes, 111
   keyboard driver routine, 127

listing of (Appendix), 195–197
   parts of, 111
Security, 165–176
   LOCK, 168–171
   LOCK.BAT, 171–172
   system for deterring tamperers, 167
   TIMER.BAT, 173–176
   UNLOCKER.BAT, 172–173
SHELL, CONFIG.SYS file, 96
SHIFT, subcommands, batch files, 119
Slow accessing, troubleshooting, 211–212
Small computer system interface (SCSI), 22
SORT, 123–124
sorting batch file utilities, 147
Speed (affecting factors), 17–20
   access time, 19
   average latency, 19
   cylinder size, 17–18
   data transfer rate, 18–19
ST506/412 interface, 21
Storage
   floppy disks, 10–14
   making of, materials used, 11–12
   mass storage options, 63–67
     capacity and needs, 64–65, 66–67
     networked PCs, 66
     for stand-alone, 64–65, 66–67
     for word-processing, 66–67
   sizes of, 10–11
Subcommands, 107–114
Subdirectories, 84–86
   CHDIR (CD) command, 86, 87
   copying of, 90
   creation of, 87, 149
   moving through directories, 86–87
   removal of, 87, 90
   removing, 149–11
   RMDIR (RD) command, 87
   viewing contents of, 85–86, 89
System-level interfaces, 21–22

INDEX

System environment, 90–91
  prompt, redefining, 91

T

Tape cartridge storage, 46–47
  storage by files, 47
Thermo-magneto-optics (TMO)
  disk, 45
TREE Command, 88

U

UDISK.SYS file, 41
Utility menu, UTILMEN.BAT,
  179–180

V

Viewing, contents of
  subdirectories, 85–86, 89

W

Word processing, and capacity,
  66–67

X

XCOPY, 50, 190–191
XENIX, 65, 78

About the Author

DAVID D. BUSCH has been twice honored by the Computer Press Association for Best Computer Book in both the Product Specific and Fiction categories. In April 1987 his book *Secrets of MacWrite, MacPaint and MacDraw* earned top honors, while his work of computer humor, *Sorry about the Explosion*, was recognized in 1986. He is also the author of the long-running "DR. DOS" column in *PC Companion* magazine. The series, which deals with MS-DOS and hard disk tricks and tips, has been heralded by readers as the publication's most popular feature.

Over the past six years he has been a contributor to most of the major computer magazines, including *Personal Computing, Creative Computing, Microcomputing, 80 Micro*, and *Interface Age*, and has been a contributing editor and/or monthly columnist in a half-dozen magazines, including *RUN* and *Portable 100/200*. Busch has written a total of 400 articles on computer topics and has published 18 books. Five of these books have dealt with IBM-oriented topics, including the best-selling *PC-DOS Customized; Program Your IBM PC to Program Itself; The IBM PC Subroutine Cookbook; Inside Secrets of WordStar 2000;* and now *Hard Disk Solutions with Batch File Utilities.*

Busch has personally installed a broad range of hard disks, including the disk card add-ons, in computers owned by himself and associates, and has been using hard disks creatively since 1984.